"Change is hard. It can make us feel this powerful new book, my friend Andi Andrew walks us through the shifting seasons of life recognizing the hand of God even in the hardest moments. We are not alone, and we are loved."

Sheila Walsh, author and TV host

"Andi guides us to move toward acceptance and healing when we have underestimated the *bravery* it takes to deal with change—especially when we don't realize we need it or understand the why behind it, or when we underestimate the impact of it on our lives. Andi reminds us that the peace, joy, and contentment promised us through our faith in Jesus Christ is possible. We are sure to see what we may not have seen before through new lenses as Andi gives us a brilliant look into facing transition in new way."

Jimmy and Irene Rollins, authors, pastors, and founders of TWO=ONE marriage ministry

"Change comes into our lives whether we are ready or not. That's probably why people don't like it very much. But as our friend Andi reminds us, God wants us to thrive in the midst of change. Reading this book is like having a conversation with Andi, which is one of our favorite things. Don't miss it!"

Pastors Josh and Lisa Surratt, Seacoast Church

"In her new book, *Braving Change*, Andi vulnerably walks us through how beautiful change can be in our lives. She faces down the lie that change is all bad and instead shows us that we get to choose how we respond and who we become. As someone who has faced a lot of painful change, I found a lot of comfort and 'me too' moments while reading *Braving Change*. Through Andi's mixture of personal stories, reflections, and focused prayers, this book is a powerful tool for anyone who is journeying through change in their life!"

Jeni Baker, co–global executive director of Celebrate Recovery

"*Braving Change* by Andi Andrew is the book we all need as we navigate constant change, both expected and unexpected. This transformative guide explores the art of embracing and growing through change without feeling untethered. Andi's personal stories and profound wisdom will encourage you to welcome growth and trust the Lord through change, even when it doesn't make sense. This is a must-read for anyone seeking to find strength, resilience, and purpose amid life's ever-changing seasons."

Mike and Julie Signorelli, founders of V1 Church

"Change inside of us and around us is inevitable. This book offers wisdom and handlebars for how to bravely navigate our changing world by holding on to Christ, our Unchanging Rock Eternal. Andi provides practical steps that help you not only rise above the challenges but grow through them."

Meshali Mitchell, photographer, entrepreneur, podcast host

"Andi is a trusted voice in my life because I know she practices the truth she writes and speaks. *Braving Change* is no exception. Wanted or unwanted, change is a part of the human experience. But change does come with an invitation to allow it to shape our hearts, mold our thinking, and usher us closer to the heart of God. If you're ready to receive that invitation, I can't think of a better resource than *Braving Change* or a better guide than Andi Andrew to lead you through your journey."

Nicole Zasowski, marriage and family therapist
and author of *What If It's Wonderful?*

"Job promotions, a new love interest, or the birth of a miracle baby . . . some change is welcomed with open arms. But what do we do when change comes to us like a wildfire, burning away everything in its path, leaving us with the broken rubble of a dream in our hands? Andi Andrew's new book, *Braving Change*, will not only help you release control in transition but also give you the courage to trust that God is in fact working together *all* things for your good (even when it feels like the opposite). I have watched Andi celebrate victories with a wild dance party and in other seasons lay down unfulfilled promises at the feet of Jesus with faith, tear-stained cheeks, and trembling hands. I pray that as you read these pages you can confidently know that your story is going to look beautifully different, and Andi's words will help you find the strength you didn't know you had."

Jessi Green, revivalist, director of Saturate Global,
author of *Wildfires* and *Saturate*

BRAVING
CHANGE

OTHER BOOKS BY ANDI ANDREW

She Is Free

Fake or Follower

Friendship—It's Complicated

BRAVING CHANGE

RELEASE THE PAST, WELCOME GROWTH,

AND TRUST WHERE GOD IS LEADING YOU

ANDI ANDREW

BakerBooks

a division of Baker Publishing Group
Grand Rapids, Michigan

Published by Baker Books
a division of Baker Publishing Group
Grand Rapids, Michigan
www.bakerbooks.com

Printed in the United States of America

Library of Congress Cataloging-in-Publication Data
Names: Andrew, Andi, 1978– author.
Title: Braving change : release the past, welcome growth, and trust where God is leading you / Andi Andrew.
Description: Grand Rapids, Michigan : Baker Books, a division of Baker Publishing Group, [2024] | Includes bibliographical references.
Identifiers: LCCN 2023022902 | ISBN 9781540903495 (paper) | ISBN 9781540903853 (cloth) | ISBN 9781493444076 (ebook)
Subjects: LCSH: Change—Religious aspects—Christianity. | Christian life. | Change (Psychology)—Religious aspects—Christianity. | Spiritual formation.
Classification: LCC BV4599.5.C44 A45 2024 | DDC 248.4—dc23/eng/20230718
LC record available at https://lccn.loc.gov/2023022902

24 25 26 27 28 29 30   7 6 5 4 3 2 1

To the wounded (and healing) warriors, hope-filled helpers, dedicated disciples, passionate peacemakers, and loving-yet-limping leaders, this book is for you.

Stay in the race.

Paul,

there's no one else I'd rather brave the changes of life with. Even on our darkest days, I'm safe with you. You have consistently shown me the love of Jesus, and it has changed me for the better. I'm confident to face every twist and turn that comes our way because I'll be facing them beside you.

Also, to Tanya and Kaylee,

you know why.

There aren't enough pages in the world to dedicate this book to you both adequately. So for now I'll just say it again: thank you.

CONTENTS

INTRODUCTION

When you hear the word *change*, what runs through your mind? Do you batten down the hatches and prepare for the worst? Do you catastrophize and go down unhelpful rabbit holes? Do you map out how to control every outcome and every person? Or are you an adventurer who loves to sail the seas of change? Maybe even a chaser of change for another adrenaline hit? Or perhaps you're running from something, making tangible changes, like moving to a new state or changing jobs, because it seems like the lesser evil, rather than addressing what needs to be dealt with. No matter the lens you look through when you view change, endings, and transitions, the absolute truth is that God is stable and constant in and through every moment of time. He is our Rock, and, spiritually speaking, wind, waves, and storms are promised—they *will* hit us. And when they do, we'll find out just what we've built our lives on.

Change is inevitable. Take getting older, for example: Why does my body succumb to the gravitational pull when my spirit feels like it just keeps getting younger? Why do the frown lines get deeper and the laugh lines more defined? What about our kids?

I've become the person who now tells new parents, unsolicited, "Don't blink; it just goes so fast!" I often think of my parents, who've heard their stage of life called "the sunset years," likened to a season of gazing out, taking in the beauty of a day's end, while at the same time battling natural fears that arise, knowing death is closer than it used to be.

What about changes in our relationships? How come it seems like we never graduate from those high school feelings of trying to fit in and find our people? Oh, and then there's the unrelenting news feed, swirling into the center of our households, thrashing at us like currents of untamed water as we try to grip onto something—anything—unsure as to whether we may drown in the cultural tide or get stronger and swim against it. I could go on . . .

As I begin to write this book, it's the first day of my eldest son's senior year. I'm sitting here taking a moment to myself in the early hours of the morning to write out my thoughts (and big feelings) before the whirlwind of lunch-making, breakfast-eating, and morning conversations. This will most likely be followed by my yelling, "Hurry up and get in the car!" before that swift yet laden-with-opportunity-for-connection school run is in progress. This is a year of change for our family—again. I'll probably look back and read these words in the years to come and take a deep breath, remembering the highs and lows of this transitional year. Hopefully, I'll reflect, learn, grow, apologize, encourage myself, and celebrate the goodness of God amid a life truly lived, with all its nuance, including the mundane, climactic, painful, joy-filled, shocking, and even forgettable moments.

This isn't our first rodeo when it comes to change, and I'm sure you have experienced many changes as well. You might be smack-dab in the middle of a (joyful or painful) transition in life that you didn't see coming, or you could be in the midst of making some big decisions, choosing change that is going to alter the course of your life. Or maybe you've suffered a loss that has broken your heart, and you're left wondering how to pick up the pieces and move forward. Wherever you find yourself at this present moment, there's a high probability that you're holding this book in your hands because you're either in the midst of braving change and need a friend to walk alongside you or about to embark on something new and looking for a field guide to bring along on the journey.

The truth is, life is full of change: good change, painful change, disappointing change, national change, hope-filled change, uncomfortable change, natural change, political change, necessary change, traumatic change, joy-filled change, shocking change, and of course, desired change. Change is constant, and if I've learned anything along the path of life, it's that change and transition can be wonderful teachers, shaping and molding us more into the likeness of Christ. We can grow through them and rise above them, or they can take us out.

Braving change is part of life.

While the earth remains, kingdoms will continue to rise and fall. There will be wars and rumors of wars. Unstoppable pain and tragedy will ravage our fallen world, coupled with triumphant stories of hope and renewal. Our news feed will not cease until Christ returns, nor will the social commentary that comes with it. The expanding and contracting taking place on earth—the pruning, cutting off, shaking, and awakening—feel like persistent labor pangs overwhelming the senses, often causing us to either fight, fly, freeze, or fawn. We live in the now but not yet; Jesus has come to give us life and life to the full, but the enemy still prowls around like a roaring lion on our broken planet, seeking whom he may devour. Death still wreaks havoc on earth, but we are in covenant with the Life Giver, living in the tension of pain but anchored in a hope that does not disappoint us or put us to shame. And the beautiful thing is, we can grow and still live a fruitful life in and through it all.

So, how do we come out of the rubble of overwhelm and disappointment that endings and transition can bring? How do we continue to move forward and stay in love with Jesus? How do we release the past, welcome growth, and still choose to love others? How do we hold on to hope, no matter what life throws our way? How do we rise above and allow the unending turmoil around us to shape and mold us more into the likeness of Christ instead of letting it take us out? How do we trust where God is leading us when nothing looks like it used to?

The crescendo of the Sermon on the Mount in Matthew 7 speaks deeply to me every time I read it. Jesus is concluding one of the most (if not *the* most) pivotal sermons ever preached, ushering in the new covenant. He doesn't abolish the Law or the Prophets but fulfills them by His every word and deed (Matt. 5:17). He breaks down what it is to faithfully surrender our lives and follow Him in the way, from the Beatitudes to entering through the narrow gate and everything in between. Then Jesus finishes with these words:

> Therefore *everyone who hears these words of mine and puts them into practice is like a wise man who built his house on the rock*. The rain came down, the streams rose, and the winds blew and beat against that house; yet it did not fall, *because it had its foundation on the rock*. But everyone who hears these words of mine and does not put them into practice is like a foolish man who built his house on sand. The rain came down, the streams rose, and the winds blew and beat against that house, and it fell with a great crash. (Matt. 7:24–27)

Jesus's words still cry out to our hearts today: *Don't just listen and merely hear My words*—live *them!* Embody *them.* Practice *them. Build your life on them ... on the Rock.* Because change is a comin', friend, and it won't stop until His Kingdom fully comes and His will is completely done here on earth as it is in heaven.

Matthew 7:24–27 will be an anchor Scripture on the journey we're about to embark on together. So go ahead and dig deep into the whole of the Sermon on the Mount in Matthew 5–7 to gain greater richness and understanding throughout our time together. The Word is clear, and the human experience proves time and again that we're going to walk through tests and trials. But will we build on shifting sands that will wash away when the storms come? Or will we build our lives on Christ?

In this book, we're going to bravely face the changes we are in, have gone through, are trying to avoid, or are about to embark on. We're not going to look away, evade, deny, or try to control what's happening around us because we already know that we can't. We can, however, make wise, informed, surrendered, biblical decisions as we move through change one step at a time.

We're also going to dig deep and meditate on a key Scripture in each chapter and then reflect on different questions that require responses. These Scriptures and questions are an opportunity to get practical and map out some different choices we can make that will help us navigate the waters of change with more grace, trust, maturity, and hopefully more humility—because God knows we need it. Finally, I'll add a guided prayer at the end of each chapter for you to pray out loud as a jumping-off point to go deeper in your relationship with God.

My prayer for you is the same as the apostle Paul's was for the Ephesians:

> For this reason I kneel before the Father, from whom every family in heaven and on earth derives its name. I pray that out of his glorious riches he may strengthen you with power through his

Spirit in your inner being, so that Christ may dwell in your hearts through faith. And I pray that you, being rooted and established in love, may have power, together with all the Lord's holy people, to grasp how wide and long and high and deep is the love of Christ, and to know this love that surpasses knowledge—that you may be filled to the measure of all the fullness of God.

Now to him who is able to do immeasurably more than all we ask or imagine, according to his power that is at work within us, to him be glory in the church and in Christ Jesus throughout all generations, for ever and ever! Amen. (Eph. 3:14–21)

You are not alone. You are deeply loved, more than you know. May we grow in strength by the power of the Holy Spirit together as we allow the constant change around us to bring Christlike change within us. May God's grace be upon you as you begin again.

BUILDING ON THE ROCK

Scripture Meditation: Matthew 7:24–27

Therefore everyone who hears these words of mine and puts them into practice is like a wise man who built his house on the rock. The rain came down, the streams rose, and the winds blew and beat against that house; yet it did not fall, because it had its foundation on the rock. But everyone who hears these words of mine and does not put them into practice is like a foolish man who built his house on sand. The rain came down, the streams rose, and the winds blew and beat against that house, and it fell with a great crash.

Take some time to read this key Scripture out loud. Underline or write down in a journal what stands out to you and why.

I strongly encourage reading the entirety of the Sermon on the Mount (Matt. 5–7) for the context of our key verse and then write out Matthew 7:24–27 to meditate on it even more deeply.

REFLECTION QUESTIONS

- When you hear the word *change*, what runs through your mind?
- How have you coped with or walked through major or minor changes in the past, and what are you hoping to get out of this book?

GUIDED PRAYER

Father, at the start of this journey with You, I intentionally surrender all and choose to trust You. I make a conscious choice to let go of control and ask that You would lead the way. Holy Spirit, teach my heart and remind me of all truth as I navigate the changes I am walking through. Jesus, thank You for showing me the way to live, no matter what is going on around me. You truly are the way, the truth, and the life that leads me to the heart of the Father.

CHAPTER 1

THE CHANGE WE THINK WE WANT

What distinguishes the wise from the foolish? Their foundation. When the storm comes, the wise remain standing.

Bob Sorge

I love people-watching on airplanes, especially when the pilot says for the seventh time, "Ladies and gentlemen, I'm sorry to inform you that we're going to be delayed a bit longer. Air traffic control has informed us that we are not cleared for takeoff." Groans emerge from every direction, people begin texting wildly or making urgent, frustrated phone calls, and if I'm lucky, I'll get to watch someone go off and give an innocent flight attendant (who has *no* control over the delay) a piece of their ever-loving mind. I only wish each and every one of you could've been there to see my husband put his foot down and silence an unsuspecting woman from her tirade in the midst of a very long delay. This woman's sass was ruining the atmosphere for everyone within earshot.

On this particular trip, my husband and I had gotten complimentary upgrades to first class. Yes, we were separated because they were complimentary, but I could easily smile and wave at him from my seat across the aisle. I settled in, put my feet up, accepted every snack and drink the flight attendants were offering, covered myself in my cozy blanket, and started a movie. When said woman began her tirade, my husband only gave short glances her way to begin with. You know, the ones that nonverbally say, "Um, what are you doing? Social skills, please. Read the room." Nope, his irritated head turns weren't working. Every time the baby from the row in front of her made a sound, this woman stood up and made loud groaning sounds, terrifying the parents trying to soothe their newborn, causing them to do the "big bounce," sumo-squat style, working out their glutes and quads, in an effort to keep their baby calm so that this woman didn't unleash her wrath on them.

She began yelling like a schoolyard bully at the flight attendants in her purview: "You guys are lying to us! What's really going on? Tell us why we're delayed. I want to speak to the pilot, now! I need a Xanax." Her husband slunk lower and lower in his seat, communicating without words, "I'm not even with her," though we all knew he was. My husband's glances her way began to get longer, his drawn-out, frustrated breaths slower and deeper, not to mention his furrowing brow became more defined with each look. I started to giggle to myself, knowing what she had coming. So, I picked up my popcorn and took off one headphone so I could simultaneously hear my movie and watch my husband do what he was about to do.

"Okay, that's enough."

Flight attendant stops. Looks shocked, then relieved. Phones slowly lift into the air to record. Said woman is offended that someone would speak to *her*. I'm pretty sure her favorite quote is, "They whispered to her, 'You cannot withstand the storm.' She whispered back, 'I am the storm.'" She gathers herself, looks at my husband. He continues.

"*You* are more stressful than this delay."

The woman stumbles over the words that she's trying to pull from her brain to unleash out of her mouth. The words trip out of her. "Well"—as her husband looks the other way, obviously longing to disappear—"could you imagine being married to me?"

To which my husband *categorically* replies (because I'm sitting right there), "No, I could not."

Flight attendant releases the tension in her shoulders, looks to my husband, and mouths, "Thank you." Stressful woman takes her Xanax, falls asleep, and blesses the plane with peace for the duration of the flight.

The Lord spoke to me through that hilarious, overly dramatic situation in first class. We are *that* woman. We cry out for change in our lives, we run to the altar, we ask others to pray for us, we want a new season, we want Jesus to fix it, and then when God begins to move on our prayers, *or* when it seems that things are delayed, we reject all reason and begin to yell and shake our fist at the heavens. "Not this way! I mean, I know I asked for You to change my life, and I sang 'I Surrender All' last week in worship, but really, I'm partially surrendered—and You already know this because You're God. Can't You just bless my blueprint? Can You just take a look at my plans and, *voilà*, make them happen? I mean, I know You're not a genie in a bottle, but maybe You make an exception today?" When we act like this, we might as well put on an entitled-brat-Veruca-Salt accent (*Willy Wonka* reference, for those wondering) and say, "I want it, and I want it now, Daddy!" We're destroying the atmosphere around us when we're the one who asked God to change our life and take us from Point A to Point B.

This is not it. This is not a surrendered life given fully to Jesus. Listen, there is change we think we want, but when the vehicle for transformation shows up on our doorstep (e.g., things start shifting around us, or people leave, or the obvious grace to complete even a difficult task or assignment lifts, or we get fired, or a pandemic hits, or we move cities, or we get sick, or we lose a loved one unexpectedly, or national unrest and division confront us), what do we do? Do we start to fight anyone in proximity? Do we go into flight mode and pretend it's not happening, disappearing into a happy place in our mind or self-medicating? Do we freeze, unable to make any rational decisions in order to move forward and make progress? Or do we fawn, pleasing, appeasing, and pacifying anyone in our vicinity in order to keep ourselves safe from further perceived harm or unrest?

For the sake of the illustration, airplanes are vehicles of transition and change. They take us from where we are to where we're going, and in the long, drawn-out, sometimes-filled-with-delays middle is where we get to see what we're made of, whether we like it or not. They simply show us what comes out of us when we can't fully control what's going on around us (e.g., weather delays or other unruly, annoying passengers who put their elbows on *your* armrest, chew with their mouth open, snore loudly on your shoulder, or don't discipline their disobedient children).

Am I, or are you, that woman?

Pause and reflect before we move forward. First, where have you either (1) cried out for change and it's happening in a way you wouldn't have chosen or seen coming, (2) been surprised by change but you're moving with and through it, or (3) absolutely didn't ask for the change you're in the middle of and you're still in shock? Second, like the woman on the airplane, in what ways are you possibly coping or self-protecting? Before we move ahead, take some time to write out where you're at on the next page.

_____

_____

_____

_____

_____

_____

_____

_____

NEW SEASONS

We're suckers for new things: new trends, new shows, new material things, you name it. If we're not careful, this sneaks into our Christianity as materialism and entitlement. Yet there's a dichotomy we live in as believers, where the Word states that "there is nothing new under the sun" (Eccles. 1:9) and that God *makes all things new* or that He's doing a new thing (Isa. 43:19). I mean, we love the idea of new seasons, don't we? God clearly uses earthly seasons as a type and shadow of what takes place in our lives while we live on planet earth. "While the earth remains, seedtime and harvest, cold and heat, summer and winter, day and night, shall not cease" (Gen. 8:22 ESV). So when we step into a new season, whether that's a new job, a new city, a new relationship or friendship, new depths in our intimacy with God, obedience in our calling, a new adventure, getting married, having children, or whatever you've named above, we can often be a bit taken aback by the pathway laid out before us. Because in our hearts, we've already planned out our own way, but the Lord has been determining our steps and continues to do so (Prov. 16:9). His perspective is vaster than we can imagine, and it's eternal, whether we perceive it or not.

Israel cried out for deliverance, for a "new season" in their promised land as God's chosen people. I'm not sure they saw Moses coming or would've chosen him as their leader and deliverer. You know, the Hebrew boy who was rescued by Pharaoh's daughter in the middle of a genocide as he floated down the river in a basket. He grew to become a man in the very palace that oppressed his own people, but he was separate from them, lacking any understanding of what it was to be under the heavy weight of slavery. And then in Moses's first documented public move to stand up for his people, he murdered an Egyptian who was beating one of his own. They in turn rejected his help, calling him a murderer (because he was) and causing him to flee to Midian to live in exile for forty years. It was in the place of exile that God spoke to him through the burning bush, telling him to go back to Egypt and deliver his people (Exod. 2–3).

The assignment given to him was not an easy one. We read that for forty years Moses's people raged against his leadership, and ultimately the plan of God, when God was in the midst of answering their prayers to be delivered from their oppressors. It seems to me that they wanted it to be done another way, and often we're the same. We long for the days of old while asking for something new at the same time, choosing stubbornness instead of surrender.

In Exodus 16:1–4, the Israelites complain about how God is delivering them into their new season.

> They set out from Elim, and all the congregation of the people of
> Israel came to the wilderness of Sin, which is between Elim and

Sinai, on the fifteenth day of the second month after they had departed from the land of Egypt. And the whole congregation of the people of Israel grumbled against Moses and Aaron in the wilderness, and the people of Israel said to them, "Would that we had died by the hand of the LORD in the land of Egypt, when we sat by the meat pots and ate bread to the full, for you have brought us out into this wilderness to kill this whole assembly with hunger."

Then the LORD said to Moses, "Behold, I am about to rain bread from heaven for you, and the people shall go out and gather a day's portion every day, that I may test them, whether they will walk in my law or not." (ESV)

This passage is rich and worthy of reflection. Funnily enough, I can remember reading it while on a plane on my way to a speaking engagement. My husband and I were in the middle of a transition, and God clearly spoke to me through His Word. He then whispered, *Andi, you've cried out for Me to change your life, and I am. But now all you're doing is complaining about what you don't have in this new season. You're crying out for your figurative meat pots when I want to deliver you and give you your promised land. You get to choose how you walk this out.*

Do you love a good wake-up call like this? I am always so grateful for a loving warning. The truth of the matter is, God said that He was about to provide food for the Hebrew people by raining down bread from heaven. God has bread from heaven for us, but as long as we hunger for the meat pots of the past, it's hard to see and feast on God's goodness and provision in the present.

We're comfortable with the meat pots of the past because at least they were predictable, reliable even. Yet somewhere deep down we also know that staying enslaved to our past and pain is dangerous and detrimental, not just to us but also to those around us. If we want something new, we'll surely come face-to-face with ourselves in the desert seasons like the Israelites did, understanding the areas of our lives where we need to be healed, strengthened, encouraged, and changed because there will be giants to confront in the new land God desires to give us. If we genuinely want something new, transitional seasons are essential to form our character for what is needed in the weeks, months, and years to come.

DIDN'T SEE THAT COMING

Have you ever said the words, "I didn't see that coming"? Yeah, me too. You'd think I would've learned by now to keep my mouth shut. Here's a little timeline of breadcrumbs that the Lord kindly left for me to help me see "that" coming:

Day after Christmas, 2019: After our basement flooded due to a crack in the foundation, I was standing in the water trying to sop it up with all the towels we had in our house, and I heard the Lord say, *I am fixing the cracks and leaks in the foundation of the church.* I took a deep breath and side-eyed the Lord, with countless questions coming to mind. (More on this prophetic word later, in chapter 5.)

Delta lounge, March 14, 2020: I heard the Holy Spirit whisper, *Be in the Gospels, Andi. You're going to need to remember what it is to follow Jesus.* I was on one of the last flights back to NYC before the "two-week" lockdown.

Just a couple months earlier, on **New Year's Day, 2020**, these were the words whispered to my heart as I leaned in to get a word for the year: *I'm going to show you what true joy is, Andi. Read James 1.* (Puts seat belt on.)

But seriously—have you read James 1? Trials, testing, the choice to persevere? Can that be a word for someone else? We all know now that the world was about to enter a season that would shake everything we all believed to the core. It would prune and cut off everything that wasn't bearing any fruit in our lives. Ferocious spiritual storms would come and go with gale-like winds that would separate the wheat from the chaff. Lines would be drawn in the sand, relationships would be fractured, the fire of God would refine and renew, people would be "canceled," and it would become obvious who stood on the rock of Jesus Christ and who stood on the shifting sands of popular opinion, false gods, social commentary, false prophetic words, and cultural tides. It would be a year (or two or three) that would drastically change the landscape of our lives, marriages, family dynamics, friendships, cities, and church communities.

I probably should've seen it coming. And not in some doomsday, foreboding way. God was and always is lovingly shooting up flares if we'll pay attention. I was simply in denial. I had no idea what was about to go down. None of us did. Change was in the air, and the swirl had already begun.

Certain moments in time and history open all kinds of spiritual doors and reveal what's truly going on in the hearts of humans, shifting the trajectory of nations and family lines. In recent history, over the last one hundred years or so, WWI, the Great Depression, WWII, Vietnam, the Civil Rights Movement, 9/11, 2020, the passing of Queen Elizabeth II in 2022 (to name a few) all marked moments of historical change. God can only heal what is revealed, acknowledged, and repented of, and we can only change once we truly see. Sometimes things need to be laid bare to expose what needs to be rebuilt and replanted after the shaking, uprooting, and tearing down take place.

Change can come in strange ways, hard ways even, but as we see throughout Joseph's life in the book of Genesis, God always has a plan to take the things that the enemy has meant for evil and turn them around for good (Gen. 50:20).

Joseph was thrown in a pit and sold into slavery by his very own brothers after arrogantly sharing his prophetic dreams at the wrong time. Not long after, he was wrongly accused of rape in his slave master's house and sent to prison, only to rise and become a leader within that prison through a prophetic gift of dream interpretation. He was then sent to a palace where he began to interpret the dreams of the king, which propelled him into a new position where he became second-in-command of the nation, ruling with divine wisdom that saved the people throughout a seven-year famine. When his brothers came to him in need of food for survival, completely unaware that they stood before the brother they'd rejected and sold into slavery, Joseph said, "And now, do not be distressed and do not be angry with yourselves for selling me here, because it was to save lives that God sent me ahead of you. For two years now there has been famine in the land, and for the next five years there will be no plowing and reaping. But God sent me ahead of you to preserve for you a remnant on earth and to save your lives by a great deliverance" (Gen. 45:5–7). What blows me away is the eternal picture here. Joseph's pain, rejection, opposition, trial, and ultimate ability to overcome and trust God through it all saved the twelve tribes of Israel, including the tribe of Judah, which Jesus Christ would come from (see Gen. 37–50). Joseph went from pride to a pit, to a prison, and then a palace. As circumstances changed around him, the pride within him was shaped into humility as he realized God was using his life to "preserve a remnant" and save his people "by a great deliverance."

There will be profoundly personal circumstances, pivotal moments, and historical shaking that we don't see coming. They could be deeply private or feel like they're a million miles outside your sphere of influence or care. I'll say it again: I've come to understand that the constant change around us, whether it's happening in our home, corporately, or nationally, has the potential to change us for the better. Transitions in life can teach us or take us out, and the acceptance of the constant change around us always has the potential to bring Christlike change within us.

MAYBE WE SHOULD'VE SEEN IT COMING

The verses below are from the very mouth of Jesus, prophetically describing events that will take place between Jesus's prophecy in Matthew 24 and the end of the age. People have been predicting the end times throughout every generation, only to be disappointed that Jesus didn't rip through the clouds in their lifetime. Since the resurrection of Christ, we have been living in the "last days," and Jesus says that the day and hour of His return is unknown even to Him: "But about that day or hour no one knows, not even the angels in heaven, nor the Son, but only the Father" (Matt. 24:36). All we can do is choose to live as those who build their lives upon the Rock, wide awake and in love with Jesus, deciding daily to abide in Him come what may. Remember, the verses below are only a snippet of an entire book, so please take some time on your own to read the whole of it in context.

> Jesus answered: "Watch out that no one deceives you. For many will come in my name, claiming, 'I am the Messiah,' and will deceive many. You will hear of wars and rumors of wars, but see to it that you are not alarmed. Such things must happen, but the end is still to come. Nation will rise against nation, and kingdom against kingdom. There will be famines and earthquakes in various places. All these are the beginning of birth pains." (vv. 4–8)

If you ask me, we're smack-dab in the middle of the birth pains, and we have been since Jesus's resurrection. Our time on earth is nothing special in the sense that it's always been a bit wild out there, hence our deep need for Jesus.

We've got false prophets and messiahs, wars and rumors of wars, nation rising against nation, kingdom against kingdom, and dare I say, at times church against church, even though we are one body. There are famines, earthquakes, and devastation. We encourage that which needs to be corrected and sacrifice that which should be treasured and nurtured.

Jesus goes on to say,

Then you will be handed over to be persecuted and put to death, and you will be hated by all nations because of me. At that time many will turn away from the faith and will betray and hate each other, and many false prophets will appear and deceive many people. Because of the increase of wickedness, the love of most will grow cold, but the one who stands firm to the end will be saved. And this gospel of the kingdom will be preached in the whole world as a testimony to all nations, and then the end will come. (vv. 9–14)

It's clear that persecution and betrayal will happen and has been happening since Jesus roamed the earth. There will be hatred toward believers; many will turn away from the faith. There will be an increase of wickedness, causing the love of most to grow cold. Through all of this, a need to stand firm will be essential. And, not to be missed, *the gospel*, the very good news of the Kingdom, will be preached in all the world!

Election seasons, national tragedies, division in beliefs, unfaithfulness, loss, personal battles, and painful news headlines will continue to grip us like waves battering the shores of our lives. The probability that such things will draw even more lines in the sand, breaking up families and friendships, will always be heart-wrenching. What kills me in all of this is that we live like these kingdoms (little *k*) will last forever, and they simply won't. They will have an end, and yet we bow down to our political and personal idols and our cultural kings, not to mention winds and waves of doctrine that shove a wedge into the middle of our relationships with one another and our intimacy with Jesus, the actual King of Kings whose Kingdom will never end.

> To him who loves us and has freed us from our sins by his blood and made us a kingdom, priests to his God and Father, *to him be glory and dominion forever and ever. Amen.* (Rev. 1:5–6 ESV)

> Then the seventh angel blew his trumpet, and there were loud voices in heaven, saying, "*The kingdom of the world has become the kingdom of our Lord and of his Christ, and he shall reign forever and ever.*" (Rev. 11:15 ESV)

We live dangerously when we become consumed by the cares of this world, existing with a temporal mindset when there is a bigger play at hand. We are called more deeply to be trained (if we have eyes to see, ears to hear, and a heart to understand) to reign and rule as a kingdom of priests under the authority and dominion of the Lord Jesus Christ forever and ever. As we follow Jesus, what can be shaken will continue to be shaken, and our lives will be pruned; some things will be cut off so that we can bear even more fruit. (See Heb. 12:25–29; John 15.)

SO, NOW WHAT?

There have been so many times in my life when I've said, "How did I get here?" or "Why is this happening?" Probably because we think that if we do everything right according to our own righteousness, no pain or tragedy will come upon us. Sometimes it's hard to accept the fact that we live on planet earth and that it can be painful down here. Considering this reality, we have to ask ourselves, Will we make the decision to stop living in denial, face where we're at, and humbly ask God what is the best way *through*? Maybe we need to cry out for a greater understanding of grace and mercy. It's possible we need to surrender and let go of a few things or simply walk in obedience to what God has already asked us to do.

I love the song "Firm Foundation" by Cody Carnes, Chandler Moore, and Austin Davis. It speaks of how Christ is our firm foundation, the Rock that we can confidently stand on. That even when things all around us are shaken, we've never been "more glad" *because* we've chosen to put our faith in Jesus. Shaking is actually the worst, but when we build our lives on the Rock, on a God who simply won't fail us, well, it's always a good choice.

Remember Matthew 7:24–27? Will we be wise or foolish builders? "The adjectives *wise* and *foolish* describe a person's spiritual and moral state, not his intellect. Whether one is considered wise or foolish is determined by his response to Jesus's teaching."[1]

Listen, there is the change we think we want, and in the depths of our soul I imagine that we truly do want it, even when it's difficult. I don't believe that there's a single one of us who wants to become sour, stubborn, and unteachable with age. We don't dream of becoming crotchety old men or women who sit on our front porches yelling at the neighbors, gossiping about our friends, or drinking ourselves into a stupor to forget. No, we want to grow, walk in the transformational power of the Holy Spirit, and take new ground as we become more like Christ. So when we do cry out for the change we think we want, we must remember to surrender all.

Let's reflect on a quote from M. Scott Peck:

Life is difficult. This is a great truth, one of the greatest truths. It is a great truth because once we truly see this truth, we transcend it. Once we truly know that life is difficult—once we truly understand and accept it—then life is no longer difficult. Because once it is accepted, the fact that life is difficult no longer matters.[2]

Don't look for the path of least resistance. Trust me, you won't grow there. Count the cost of change. Remember when you cry out for something new, there will be a price to pay, so weigh it and then pay it. If you're walking through a loss that you didn't see coming, may I encourage you to lift your eyes and see the way through with our very good God as your Comforter and Helper? Let Him shelter you under the shadow of His wings. Let Him provide for you, love you, heal you, and hold you. You will see better days and, dare I say, the goodness of God in the land of the living.

BUILDING ON THE ROCK

Scripture Meditation: Exodus 16:1–4 ESV

They set out from Elim, and all the congregation of the people of Israel came to the wilderness of Sin, which is between Elim and Sinai, on the fifteenth day of the second month after they had departed from the land of Egypt. And the whole congregation of the people of Israel grumbled against Moses and Aaron in the wilderness, and the people of Israel said to them, "Would that we had died by the hand of the LORD in the land of Egypt, when we sat by the meat pots and ate bread to the full, for you have brought us out into this wilderness to kill this whole assembly with hunger."

Then the LORD said to Moses, "Behold, I am about to rain bread from heaven for you, and the people shall go out and gather a day's portion every day, that I may test them, whether they will walk in my law or not."

Take some time to consider where you've cried out to God for change and then grumbled because of how it's come to pass.

REFLECTION QUESTIONS

- What figurative meat pots are you longing for while God is trying to move you on and do something new?
- Where can you see "bread from heaven" (i.e., God's provision and kindness) where maybe you've been missing it because you've been too fixated on the past?

GUIDED PRAYER

Father, I trust You, yet deep down I long to trust You even more. Change me from the inside out, Lord, and reveal the parts of me that are fearful or resistant to these changes so that I can willingly surrender all. Ultimately, I want to become more like You, Jesus. Help me, Holy Spirit, to know what to let go of, what to hold on to, and what to pick up. Reveal to me the areas in my heart where I am being stubborn and where I need healing. I lay my life at Your feet.

CHAPTER 2

RECOGNIZE TRANSITION WHEN YOU'RE IN IT

Your life is a story of transition. You are always leaving one chapter behind while moving on to the next.

Anonymous

I once got into a fight with a washing machine. True story.

We'd just moved into a new apartment in Brooklyn that had come with a washer and dryer. Now, if you have ever lived in New York City or one of her boroughs, you know just how big a deal it is not to have to lug your wash down the street to a laundromat (with a family of six, that's a literal nightmare) or share a washer and dryer with a host of other people in your building who may or may not respect your clothing if you leave it for two minutes too long in the washer. You know, the people who steal your stuff or throw it on top of the dryer without a care?

All that said, our glorious washer and dryer were put to immediate use the day we could get through the doors into our new place after we'd signed the lease. I was washing all of our bedding, pillow covers, big blankets, and towels—all the bulky items. At some point in the washing of all of the things, I went to check on where the washer was in its cycle, and that's when the fight broke out. As I came down the stairs, all I heard was a heavy *thud, thud, thud, thud, thud,* and then . . . nothing. Complete silence. The washer had stopped working altogether, and a warning light incessantly blinked, sending the message that it was off-balance. I opened the lid, moved the bedding around so it was evened out, and put the spin cycle back on. But, oh no, it didn't start to spin— it started to fill with water, adding more time that I hadn't allowed for to my perfectly planned-out day. Thirty minutes later, I came back down to the same *thud, thud, thud* sound and felt heat begin to rise like a furious air bubble about to burst in my chest. I was actually angry at the washer. The same thing happened again, and in my stubbornness I tried one more time to get the spin cycle to work. But no, it filled with water *again,* setting me back even further in my precious schedule, and I lost it. I raised my arms in the air, palms open, and in a fit of fury yelled from the depths of my gut and slammed both palms down on the washing machine while it continued to defiantly fill with water. I saw the feet of one of my children start to come down the stairs, then swiftly turn around to avoid the ferocity they must have felt emanating from the depths of my soul toward a washing machine. Yes, a *washing machine.*

I wish that were the end of the story, but it's not. Right then and there I started to sob uncontrollably, like a baby who is hungry, tired, colicky, and needs a diaper change all at once. *Why, oh why, Lord?!* (Shakes fist at the sky while tears dramatically roll down thy furious, reddened face.) I can imagine God looking at

38

me, saying, "Why *what*, Andi?" But He didn't speak to me like that; He actually nudged me tenderly and said, *You know this isn't about the washing machine, right?*

I jumped up on top of the washing machine, which was still filling with water, eliciting an eye roll, and I replied through my ugly cry, "Well then, what is this about?"

To which I heard, *You're in a major life transition, Andi, and I want to show you that I am your Father.*

The crying only got uglier as I finally understood my season. It was like I had awakened from a deep sleep in a hotel room in a city I'd never been in and finally remembered where I was. We had just lost my beautiful mother-in-law to an inoperable brain tumor, and my parents were moving to the West Coast after living next door to us for eight years, helping us pioneer, pastor, and care for Liberty Church while simply doing life with us. My world was spinning. We were losing parents—our support network—left, right, and center. I had been feeling abandoned and alone, and I hadn't even realized it.

If we don't recognize transition when we're in it, we start taking it out on unsuspecting washing machines. All jokes aside, we know that it's those who are closest to us who suffer if we don't acknowledge the changes happening to us, around us, or within us. Grief will bottle itself inside of our hearts until it erupts on someone somewhere who is unaware of the significance of what we're holding in and unable to help us or hold us like we need to be held. The Word says, "Blessed are those who mourn, for they will be comforted" (Matt. 5:4). We'll talk about grief a lot more in chapter 3, but it's good to acknowledge the areas where we're avoiding, suppressing, or bottling things up that need to be let out.

So, will we take a three-day journey or a forty-year journey? There's never been a better time than now to change your trajectory and choose to brave the changes ahead of you.

SIGNS AND TYPES OF TRANSITION

There are the signs that things need to change in your life, and then there are the signs that things are simply changing no matter what you try to do to stop it. For instance, maybe you work in a toxic environment, and there is no sign of change in leadership, culture, or structure. Or maybe the grace is lifting in a certain season of your life, and things all around you, including relationships and proximity to others, are changing at a rate beyond your control. This could also include the inevitable letting go of a child into adulthood, being left with an empty nest that you knew would come one day but aches nonetheless. Maybe your spouse whom you've been with for the majority of your life passed away, leaving a cavernous void.

It can be during these times when the enemy tries to tempt us to veer offtrack, even just slightly. If you find yourself wanting to throat-punch people more often than not, having a desire to sleep in all day, every day, experiencing constant gut issues, or lacking the desire to engage in normal, everyday life tasks, take a moment and ask yourself why. Many of these may be signs that a change is shaking up your life, and avoidance or numbness is only giving you health issues mentally, emotionally, spiritually, and physically.

Three main types of transition that we encounter are emotional, physical, and intellectual. In no particular order or category, just to name a few, these can include getting married, the death of a loved one, having a baby, any type of loss, necessary endings (fill in the blank), a prolonged sickness, or retirement. The list of changes we're potentially facing is personal and constant.

MOUNTAINTOPS, VALLEYS, AND PLATEAUS

Let's look at a few categories where our lives are shaken up by change, whether we choose it or not.

Mountaintops

Mountaintops take our breath away. These are the seasons of change that bring joy. There's an ease in praising God and letting everyone know just how good He is.

These are only a handful of mountaintop moments, but please add your own at the end of the list.

- Watching the child you prayed for be born and placed in your arms.
- Graduating after giving everything to (or surviving) your studies and—the bonus—landing a dream job in your field.
- Getting married to your best friend and having a huge celebration.
- Being born again—hands down the actual best mountaintop moment.
- Getting baptized with your family and/or church family watching and cheering you on.
- Saying yes to something you've always hoped would become an opportunity for you and being blown away that it has actually come to pass.
- Attaining financial freedom.
- Buying your first home.
- Retiring after years of hustling, sowing, and building. Maybe even planning for new adventures!
- Moving to the city or town you've always known was made for you to pour your life into.
- Finally landing that job you were born for or moving into your field of passion.
- Hitting those health goals and genuinely being proud of taking care of your body.

- Place yours here:

_____

_____

_____

Valleys

Valley changes are the gut-punch seasons, the ones we don't ask or pray for but are part of the human experience. Yes, sometimes we willingly choose to walk through a valley due to our free will, but other times we find ourselves in situations and circumstances we never thought we would end up in, and it feels like a death.

Loss of Any Kind

- Death of a father, mother, brother, sister, child, friend, spouse, extended family member, or loved one (even the death of a pet that has been deeply faithful and loving throughout the years).
- Loss of a job, dream, or future you thought you'd have.
- Retirement. Yes, this goes here too. It's the loss of a season of life you held ground in for years. And even though there's joy in retiring, the transition into it can often feel like a valley—or so I've heard.
- Loss of health and/or mobility due to age, sickness, or an accident.
- Having a miscarriage.
- Having an abortion.
- Loss of a marriage.

- Place yours here:

_____

_____

_____

Changes That Happen to Us

- Betrayal in a marriage, friendship, work relationship, or family relationship.

- Finding out a spouse has been unfaithful.

- A spouse walking out on a marriage.

- Parents' divorce.

- A family member's incarceration.

- A difficult or terminal diagnosis for ourselves or a loved one.

- A hard diagnosis for a child: ADHD, OCD, autism, sickness of any kind, any special need that requires major life changes.

- Finding out one of our children has been abused, hurt, or bullied and not having the ability to go back in time to change it but instead needing to walk through it with them.

- Any type of mental, physical, emotional, or sexual abuse.

- Church division or loss of a community we've been a part of.

- Losing a loved one.

- Being forced to move for any reason.

- Getting fired and feeling a sense of shame and loss.

- Being single when you don't want to be and all your friends are getting married. As a close friend said to me,

"It can be a deep, dark valley where you experience constant loss."

- Being slandered and gossiped about.
- Walking through debilitating and crippling physical pain.
- Ongoing infertility while others around you just keep conceiving.
- Walking through a loved one's mental health battle.
- Nursing a loved one through sickness.
- Political, economic, and cultural changes within the nation where we live.
- Going to war as a nation and all the shaking that comes with it.
- Any type of PTSD, like from a car crash or traumatic experience of any kind.
- Place yours here:

_____

_____

_____

Changes That We Choose, Good or Bad

- Quitting a job.
- Taking a new job.
- Going to college.
- Getting married.
- Getting a divorce.
- Leaving an abusive relationship.
- Being unfaithful in our marriage.

- Saying yes to being a stay-at-home mom, even though it's one of the hardest jobs. Yet it's also deeply rewarding.
- Setting a boundary in a relationship for our mental, emotional, and spiritual health.
- Familial issues that require hard conversations and boundaries.
- Getting remarried.
- Becoming a blended family.
- Moving cities or countries.
- Planting ourselves in a new church community.
- Intentionally making new friends.
- Lying, cheating, stealing, gossiping, and the like. We're changing the trajectory of not only our lives but someone else's as well.
- Place yours here:

_____

_____

_____

Plateaus

A plateau season is somewhere between a mountaintop and a valley. The yes is obvious, but the cost is felt at the same time as the joy. It can be an in-between time in life that seems to go on and on. It's a liminal space that many of us find ourselves in throughout our lifetime. Oxford Languages defines *plateau* as "a state of little or no change following a period of activity or progress."[1] A plateau may be best described as that actual time of floating in between a major change and what is next.

- Getting engaged and planning your wedding. Lots of activity and preparation, but the final, pivotal moment of exchanging vows and doing life together hasn't happened just yet.
- Having a loved one in hospice care. Holding on and letting go all at once.
- Saying yes to a new job while finishing up an old one with integrity and honor. It can feel like a drag not to be in the next season, but how we walk out the in-between is very important.
- Conceiving a child and having to wait nine months for the labor to begin, especially that last month when we feel like we're ready to burst.
- Having that beautiful baby and enjoying the season of motherhood (while being completely exhausted), but also wondering if this season will last forever. It's not rational, but it can be how we feel. Even when we hold the miracle in our arms, we can long for what's next.
- Losing a loved one and being in a season of grief while holding on to hope that better days will be ahead.
- Starting a new business with so much excitement and then hitting a plateau in sales, fundraising, or momentum. This can cause us to wonder when the next breakthrough will come as we continue daily to be faithful with what's in front of us.
- Place yours here:

_____

_____

_____

Being aware of our season helps us move into a place of acceptance and healing if we're in need of it, even if we never fully understand why the shifting or shaking is taking place. It also helps us remain present, not longing for what is next but getting the most out of the moment we're in. This is key to walking through change and transition as gracefully as possible, even though there will be twists, turns, and inevitable bumps in the road that we don't see coming.

It's also wise to ask ourselves, Am I making unnecessary changes that look good to any observer to avoid the actual changes I *need* to make? Am I avoiding hard conversations or possible confrontation by filling my time with things I don't really need to be doing? Am I being disobedient to the nudge of the Holy Spirit while doing my own thing—that, again, looks completely normal to any onlooker—knowing deep down I'm avoiding what's glaringly obvious right in front of me? As an illustration, am I moving the furniture around in my figurative house to make the space around me feel better temporarily, when everything in the entire house needs to be moved out and put into storage so we can tear up the foundation and build a new one because it's unstable and cracking?

Will we embrace transition or reject it when we see it coming? Will we be honest about where we're really at or keep avoiding it until the inevitable takes place? Will we go with the flow and welcome growth or fight it with everything we have? We get to choose.

REMEMBER, LABOR IS A PART OF LIFE

Here's something we have to understand: control is elusive. Just ask any woman who's had a birth plan, and she'll let you know.

With four natural labors under my belt, I must say bringing a child into the world is an allegory for the unstoppable change and transition that comes to all our lives, with or without warning. Once labor begins, there is no hindering its course until the child you've carried in your womb for nine months is in your arms, whether that be through natural labor or C-section. And once you take your newborn home, it alters everything. It changes who you are to the core: how you see things, how you make choices, what your priorities are, and even who your friends are.

We are completely helpless to stop the excruciating pain that comes with every contraction. Yes, epidurals are readily available, but for the sake of the illustration—and the premise of this book—let's look at this without the use of modern medicine. Let's look at this and walk through the entirety of this journey together choosing not to numb ourselves to the pain that brings change *and* new life. Just as the darkest of nights inevitably turn into the brightest of days, the human body will not stop doing what it's created to do to bring forth life. The change and transition that unavoidably happen all around us can be a vehicle for formation in Christ—if we go with it. Transition can be a teacher, or it can take us out. We get to choose.

Transition is the last part of active labor, where the baby's head is bearing down, bringing immense pressure before you have the urge to push. And the pain is the most intense physical pain I've ever felt in my life, as contraction upon contraction pummels your body like waves crashing on the shore at the height of a hurricane, decimating everything in their wake. Emotional changes also hit hard in transition. These are the moments in labor when a woman's behavior changes. Her eyes widen, and a look of fear or panic washes over her as she realizes she doesn't know what to do—or at the very least, feels unable to finish the labor that has already begun. She may feel out of control, while the urge to push becomes overwhelming, wild, and primal. This part of labor is painful and persistent. Yes, it does have an end, but when you're in it, you scream and flail, yelling things like "I can't do this. I'm going to die. Stop the pain . . . I'm not made for this . . . Someone help me . . . Give me all the drugs. I lied; natural childbirth is for the birds!" Pain in what's called "transition" in labor causes us to do and say things we don't mean and, *yes*, some things we really do mean.

So when you're near someone in the middle of transition in life, use wisdom, caution, and patience—this too shall pass. Life will come, the winds will change, and peace will set in.

What's wild is that before that baby is in your arms, you have this deep knowing that everything is about to change . . . for the good, but also things are about to get harder. There's a responsibility that is placed on your shoulders to steward that which has just been entrusted.

I've learned that physical labor is more peaceful and rhythmic when we just go with it, when we educate ourselves and come to an understanding that our bodies are actually built to do this wild thing. I've also learned through experience that fear slows labor down and can even bring it to a stop. So, when you feel the waves of change coming, don't batten down the hatches of fear and control; simply ask Jesus to be in the boat with you, showing you how to sleep in the storm as you cross from one side to the other.

Remember, what you believe matters because the rains of change will come pouring down. The streams will rise and transform the landscape of your life; the winds of ferocious storms will blow and beat against the house you've built. So, how's your foundation? Storms are inevitable just like labor, so prepare properly and recognize transition when you're in it, and don't give up as you brave the changes in front of you.

The rain came down, the streams rose, and the winds blew and beat against that house; *yet it did not fall, because it had its foundation on the rock*. (Matt. 7:25)

RECOGNIZING TRANSITION—MAKING IT PRACTICAL

Pause for a moment. Take a deep breath and do an inventory. Are you in the middle of a transition? How do you know on a practical level? Here are a few factors to weigh and measure in your season.

Are Your Relationships Naturally Changing, Even If It's Hard or Painful?

One of the things that has perplexed my glass-half-full heart over and over again is that not all relationships are for a lifetime. I mean, deep down I know this to be true, but it's still a harsh reality to face. I've heard it said that relationships are for a reason, for a season, or for a lifetime. Not all relationships are forever, and that's okay. When the shift starts to happen, pay attention to those relationships, and ask God for wisdom in what you're noticing.

Has the Grace Lifted?

At the end of our season in New York City, I found myself agitated by the regular goings-on of New York that never bothered me before: People yelling at you for no reason. Tourists standing in your way on the sidewalk, walking slowly and taking selfies, unaware of people trying to get around them. Congestion on the subway, rubbing up against strangers, armpits in faces, and smelling things you didn't wake up that morning thinking you'd smell. The cost of . . . everything. Nearly getting hit by cars as you're about to cross a street with a WALK sign. And rats. The rats, people! Coming out of the restaurant you love like they just had the nicest meal at the best table in the house. And sometimes they just walk a little too close to you on the sidewalk like they're about to jump in the Uber and share a ride with you. Nope. Done. Seething. Over it. I started confronting people more than usual—strangers and innocent (tourist) bystanders. The grace had lifted, and our season had come to an end. Ask yourself, Does it feel like the gears of your life are grinding when they used to move like a well-oiled machine? Spiritually, do you feel like you can't plow the soil anymore? Like nothing bears fruit and doing what you've done with joy in the past now seems futile?

Has the genuine grace for hard things lifted, and do you sense a release to move on?

Do You Find Temptation Is Knocking at Your Door in an Intense Manner?

I find that when we walk through an ending or transition, or are about to embark upon something new, there can be a temptation to veer off course. At times that temptation can get very loud, incessantly knocking at the door of our heart. Ask God for the way out and choose to take it. Don't allow the enemy to lie to you, confuse you, or tempt you to invite destruction into your life.

Scripture tells us, "Be sober-minded, be alert. Your adversary the devil is prowling around like a roaring lion, looking for anyone he can devour" (1 Pet. 5:8 CSB). Even as Jesus taught us how to pray, He said, "And forgive us our debts, as we also have forgiven our debtors. And do not bring us into temptation, but deliver us from the evil one" (Matt. 6:12–13).

Right before Jesus began His public ministry, He was baptized and then entered the desert to fast and pray for forty days. During that time, He was tempted by the devil in the desert (Matt. 4:1–11). The intensity of the temptation was intentional by the devil in an attempt to get the Savior of the world to concede His plan and bow to the enemy. Thank God (literally) that He didn't give up and give in!

Temptation is a distraction intended to lead us off the path of righteousness and onto the path of destruction. Remember, temptation is not sin—there is always a way out (1 Cor. 10:13). Stay the path.

Is Spiritual Warfare or Resistance Heightened?

Ephesians 6:12 says, "For we are not fighting against flesh-and-blood enemies, but against evil rulers and authorities of the unseen world, against mighty powers in this dark world, and against evil spirits in the heavenly places" (NLT). But when warfare of any kind gets tangibly heightened in our lives, it often comes in the form of difficulty with people. In those moments, it can seem like countless roadblocks or detours keep getting put in our way. Liminal spaces are corridors to new seasons, new hope, and promises not yet fulfilled. There is zero chance that the enemy of our soul wants us to get to the other side of what we're walking through. Stay on your knees and keep going.

Do You Find Yourself Dreaming Again (Not Escapism, but Finding Hope Afresh)?

When a dream has died, loss has shaken you, or a season has ended, grieving is so deeply important. But when you start to dream about new things—new jobs, spaces, places, relationships, and endeavors—it can be a sign of new hope on the horizon. In this space, it's wise to ask for discernment and/or simply be honest with ourselves to know the difference between escapism and a shift in assignment. One takes responsibility while the other avoids it altogether. Restlessness can ignite the flames to dream about new adventures; just be careful that you're not avoiding your reality, hard conversations, or issues within your own heart that need attention.

Is Emotional Fatigue a Constant Companion?

Pay attention when the things that used to energize you no longer do. Emotional fatigue can come as a result of mismanaged stress from our work or personal lives, and the fruit can be lack of sleep, feeling stuck, lack of energy, and so on. It's not always a sign that we need to change jobs or move on from a season; we may just need to change our rhythms. Again, you will need discernment to know the difference here.

Are the "Three Ps"–Place, People, Purpose–Aligned?

These may change several times in life, so don't be alarmed! But look around. Are you in the *place* God has called you to? Are you in constant communion and community with "your *people*"? And are you walking in your *purpose*? Another way of looking at this is knowing our *assignment*, *calling*, and *identity*. Throughout life, our assignment will change. We can look at our calling like a common thread that moves throughout each assignment with us we can't seem to get away from it because it is innate within us. And last, our identity is stable in Christ, no matter where we are or what we do. But to recognize transition when we're in it, we have to accept that our assignment is changing.

DON'T FIGHT IT–FIND YOUR NEW RHYTHM

I love dancing at weddings. Like, sweat-until-you-can't-sweat-no-more sort of dancing at weddings. When the DJ starts to play a song I can't refuse, I'll say goodbye to my husband, who's usually caught in a meaningful conversation with someone, and I'll hit the dance floor. Two out of my four kids will usually join me while the others giggle at my lack of care for what others think.

I also love to people-watch at weddings. For the most part, whether you have any sense of rhythm or not, weddings are a place where people feel free to dance with reckless abandon, even if they have no clue what they're doing. When the DJ plays "Y.M.C.A.," everyone pretty much knows what to do, even the toddlers. When the "Cupid Shuffle" comes on, again, *most* people know what to do—*most*. "Shut Up and Dance" will almost always get all of my kids on the dance floor. Oh, and when "Dancing Queen" comes on, every woman knows that the song is about her, obviously. Don't even talk to me about how "Single Ladies" causes every single woman in the house to become Beyoncé's backup dancer, proudly declaring, "If you liked it then you should have put a ring on it," while mildly glaring at a certain man in the crowd. But when a slow song comes on, have you ever watched someone totally miss the cue? They're still doing the robot to "Shut Up and Dance" while Ed Sheeran has women swooning, laying their heads on their partners' chests, moving together in a slow and steady sway. The DJ has changed the music, but your friend Sharon just can't let go of the robot, and she looks awkward.

This is what we look like when we can't find the *rhythm of grace* in the new season we're stepping into. We keep trying to do new things the old way, and we look like someone without a clue doing the "Cupid Shuffle," awkward and alone, to a slow song at a wedding.

Matthew 11:29–30 in The Message says,

> Are you tired? Worn out? Burned out on religion? Come to me. Get away with me and you'll recover your life. I'll show you how to take a real rest. Walk with me and work with me—watch how I do it. *Learn the unforced rhythms of grace.* I won't lay anything heavy or ill-fitting on you. Keep company with me and you'll learn to live freely and lightly.

If we're to understand what walking in our rhythm of grace looks like, we first have to understand grace altogether. "Grace, in Christian theology, [is] the spontaneous, unmerited gift of the divine favour in the salvation of sinners, and the divine influence operating in individuals for their regeneration and sanctification."[2]

Also, "(in Christian belief) the free and unmerited favor of God, as manifested in the salvation of sinners and the bestowal of blessings."[3]

So, Jesus extends grace to us, through His life, death, and resurrection, in the gift of salvation that we simply do not deserve by our own ability or virtue. It's unmerited favor because God so deeply loved each and every one of us in our mess and sin that He sent Jesus to redeem our lives and draw us close. And Jesus willingly laid down His life so that we could live. Simply put, His grace brings us new life. And when He gives and increases His grace for a season or situation, there is ease and favor to move within it, no matter the mountains or valleys we encounter.

Imagine with me for a moment your life as your favorite playlist. Each song is different, bringing up various memories and emotions. When the song shifts, so does the rhythm. You don't try to sing another song's lyrics when said song is blaring through the speakers. You're fully in the moment, yell-singing with everything you have, completely abandoned to the lyrical genius of one of your favorite songs.

With that said, have you ever been in a place in your life where it suddenly seemed like nothing was working like it used to? Where the metaphorical song over your life was hitting different, and not in a good way? But even though it may have been difficult to do, you had the grace to walk through it and accomplish what was in front of you? I remember a time like this when we knew our time in New York was wrapping up. We had lived there for nearly twelve years, and I loved (most) everything about pastoring, leading, and raising a family there—even the hard stuff, because I was confident we were living in our grace. In our training to plant churches, I heard someone say, "Pastoring is like a Dickens novel. It's the best of times and worst of times all in one day." This couldn't be truer. So, when the grace started to lift and the transition began to roll out for our family, as I mentioned earlier, I found myself getting angrier and angrier at things that had never really bothered me before. I started to notice that the things that hadn't been a big deal to me were increasingly becoming an annoying, big deal. Any problem that came up with pastoring human beings (this is literally the job) started to cause anger to bubble up within me instead of propelling me to humble myself and press into God for wisdom. Our time was up, the grace was lifting, and the song over our lives was changing.

The English Standard Version of Matthew 11:29–30 says it this way:

> Take my yoke upon you, and learn from me, for I am gentle and lowly in heart, and you will find rest for your souls. For my yoke is easy, and my burden is light.

If you've never seen a yoke in real life, it's a wooden beam used between a pair of oxen to help them bear the load they carry while working together. It distributes the load equally as they pull heavy objects, like a plow through hardened soil. Sometimes the yoke is also put on a single ox, once again to distribute the weight properly across its shoulders to get the work done. Jesus is telling us that His yoke is easy and His burden is light, meaning His grace upon us distributes the weight of what we're carrying evenly so that we can fulfill the task at hand *with* Him. When a particular yoke of grace lifts off our lives and we knowingly or unknowingly put on an ill-fitting one, things become difficult quickly.

Embracing transition once we recognize it in our lives will bring peace even in the midst of storms. We've got to first acknowledge where we're really at and then ask ourselves where we're avoiding or denying the inevitable.

BUILDING ON THE ROCK

Scripture Meditation: Matthew 7:25

The rain came down, the streams rose, and the winds blew and beat against that house; yet it did not fall, because it had its foundation on the rock.

How does this section of Matthew 7 land on you when it comes to recognizing transition when you're in it? What do you see that you haven't seen before, and how can you accept the reality that the storms of transition are inevitable in your life?

REFLECTION QUESTIONS

- Where is the rhythm of grace in your life right now? Where has Jesus's yoke been easy and His burden been light on the greatest and hardest days?
- Ask yourself, Where am I making physical changes to my life and/or sabotaging good things to avoid the God-breathed or, honestly, just logical changes I need to make? In other words, Where am I avoiding or denying the inevitable or simply being disobedient to the Holy Spirit's nudge?

GUIDED PRAYER

God, I thank You that You are always with me and that You are good in and through every season, even when what I am facing may be difficult. Holy Spirit, I ask that You'd enlighten me to the transition that I am presently in and possibly avoiding or denying. Be my Helper and Counselor as I choose to walk through it with humility and integrity to the best of my ability. Jesus, I lay my life down once again and let go of all the things that I fear or want to control. I thank You that I can walk in Your resurrection life daily while I intentionally build my life on You and Your love for me.

CHAPTER 3

THE NEED TO GRIEVE AND GIVE YOURSELF PERMISSION TO CHANGE

Grieving is a necessary passage and a difficult transition to finally letting go of sorrow—it is not a permanent rest stop.

Dodinsky

Grief lasts longer than you want, lingers where you don't ask it to, and shows up in unexpected moments like an uninvited guest. Yet to welcome it is to welcome deep and real healing. I find that it always seems to hit when we least expect it.

On January 6, 2022, at 3:40 p.m. (yes, I took a picture so I have the date and time), I broke down in front of Court Street Bagels. I never would've thought walking past a bagel shop in Brooklyn would've caused me to boohoo cry in front of God and everyone in Cobble Hill, but it did. And it wasn't just any bagel shop; it was the one I had gone to in joyous celebration after I found out in an ultrasound that our fourth child was another glorious son. This is one of those bagel shops in Brooklyn that is *so* good that on the weekends, a line of weary New Yorkers in need of their carb quota for the day stretches out the door and wraps around the block.

When my crying ensued, I was walking home after running errands in downtown Brooklyn. We were just under two months out from moving our family from the Northeast to the South after twelve years of sowing our lives in the city and raising our kids there. It was all they knew, and these people had become our home. I was a tad nervous because I hadn't felt much of anything about the move yet and wondered when the grief wave would hit my body. Until it did, I simply got into a mode of getting stuff done as well as monitoring the needs (emotional and physical) of my husband and four children because those were the rational things to do.

Sometimes it's just easier in times of massive change or painful loss to focus on everyone and everything else because it doesn't feel like the right time or the safe thing to do to go into a place of grieving just yet. We may actually remain in a place of denial, doing, and/or performing because burying the pain of grieving when we don't want to deal with it becomes like a drug. We become addicted to it like it's a substance that's saving us, yet it's slowly becoming a destructive place to live, ravaging our heart and soul, while the grief is still stored up in our bodies just waiting to come out. And trust me, it will come out somewhere, some way, sometime, and usually when we least expect it. This is why, in times of great change, transition, loss, and grief, we have to be gentle with ourselves, allowing time and space for us to move *through* grief, even when we wish it would just be over and done with so that we can get on with our lives. The truth is, we'll never be the same after certain moments in time, and grief is biblical and brings wholeness and life, even though it's painful to walk through.

In the previous chapter I mentioned Matthew 5:4, which says, "Blessed are those who mourn, for they will be comforted." The Comforter, the Holy Spirit, ministers to us when we mourn. Maybe you don't feel held or seen in this season and the greatest thing you can do is go into your room, shut the door, give yourself permission to let the pain out, and turn on the emotional faucet you've been scared to touch. It may start as a trickle or a steady stream, or come out like the forceful waters from a fire hose, but give yourself space and permission to go there. Lament, cry, ask all your why questions of God. Shake your fist at the sky, curl up in a ball and cry, or punch a pillow with shouts and screams. Do whatever it takes to let the grief out of your bones so that the One who conquered death can remind you that He is present in the midst of your pain. He has the ability to hold space for you when no one else does.

What have you lost? What have you let go of because to do so was the healthiest—if hardest—decision to make? Where do you need the Comforter to comfort you? Go back to your notes from chapter 2 and sit with your reality in the presence of God. Don't rush—give yourself time and space for the Holy Spirit to minister to you, spirit, soul, and body.

BELIEVE IT OR NOT, GRIEF IS A GIFT

Grief isn't a onetime event; we move *through* grief. My hope for this chapter is that I can be a loving advocate to help you move through it, while also realizing as I write these words that grief is profoundly personal and messy in nature.

William Cowper says, "Grief is itself a medicine."[1] It is for the heartsick, to bring healing, hope, wholeness, and peace. It is a gift given to us by God to pour out the hurt, pain, and loss that have been bottled up within the caverns of our heart for days, weeks, months, or years. Withholding our tears *can* cause a physical ache that can pull us into the recesses of depression. Often when we don't grieve, a bitter dullness sets in as we disconnect our bodies from the pain to stay "safe," repelling help or even love from anyone who desires to come alongside us. Healing truly comes when we get to a place of acceptance for what we've lost, even though it's difficult.

As a friend and I talked about the shocking loss of her father, she said that when she went to visit her mom about a year after his death, they started moving his clothes and ties out of his room, and as she did this simple task, she found herself in a pool of tears. It was a moment of closure as she let some of his earthly things go. This same friend had also moved from New York City to Nevada due to difficult circumstances right around the time her father passed away. The double loss felt insurmountable to her as she navigated the waters of grief like a sailor on a ship facing a storm she hadn't seen coming at that stage of her life. She told me that the simple act of getting a Nevada driver's license had been tremendously emotional: it brought a moment of resolve that caused relief and grief to wash over her all at once, inviting wholeness from a bitterly broken situation. She reminded me that seemingly simple acts of closure can also help us to come to a place of acceptance in the many stages of grief.

So, what do we do when grief feels like our ride or die? You may or may not have heard of the seven stages of grief before. So, as a refresher or maybe for the first time, let's look at them together to better understand where we may find ourselves or a loved one in the seven stages of grief.

The following are the seven stages of grief according to Better Help.com:[2]

1. **Shock and Denial:** In this stage, we can feel detached from reality, watching our life unfold like a movie, in pure disbelief that the loss or trauma has actually happened to us. Our emotions are often raw, unbridled, unexpected, and uncontrollable. We may lose sleep, feel sick, not want to eat, eat too much, try to numb with various vices, or even operate in disbelief or panic, without a logical path forward. In this stage we are usually undone.

2. **Pain and Guilt:** When the numbness fades, the pain and reality of the situation begin to set in. This is when your heart physically aches, and your emotions are wild. You may even say things like, "If only . . . ," or "If I would've just said . . . ," or "If I could've been there . . . ," or "I wish I would have . . . ," trying to go back in time and prevent the loss or major life change from taking place the way it did. This is a tender place that we have to be careful not to numb because feeling these feelings is a healthy part of the grieving and healing process.

3. **Anger and Bargaining:** These are the "shake my fist in the air at God and ask for another way" moments in the grieving process. Our anger may be directed at others, at ourselves, or even at God. We may become explosive when we are normally peaceful people. Longing for a different outcome, we may ask God why He didn't prevent the loss or the pain from coming our way. In this stage, all the questions we cannot, or may not ever, find satisfactory answers to come out of hiding and into the light.

4. **Depression, Reflection, and Loneliness:** This is the stage where we need to intentionally bring people close when all we want to do is withdraw and be all up in our feelings—alone. This is the stage where the reality of our

current situation comes crashing down. We reflect on the loss and what life will look like moving into a new season without a particular person or a certain job, city, or community of people, depending on the acute loss or change. It is imperative that we get time alone with God to really be honest with Him, while also reaching out to say what we need to say to the close circle of friends we *do* have in our world. Don't forget to lift your eyes and remember who *is* willing to be there for you and make the powerful choice to let them in.

5. **The Upward Turn:** These are the days when you actually want to get out of bed, meet with a friend, eat a good meal, exercise, do something meaningful, or simply go on a walk and feel the sunshine on your face. The upward turn happens when you realize you're having good days here and there again, walking in God-given joy without guilt, sadness, or heaviness. This is the "I think I may have turned a corner" stage of the grieving process.

6. **Reconstruction and Working Through:** Imagine having been through a destructive earthquake, and your home was demolished. In the aftermath, when it's safe to go back through the site to find valuables and see what's salvageable, you begin to see what's possible to rebuild and where you may need to just start over. As we work through our grief, we have to look through the wreckage and ask God what and how we can reconstruct with Him. This stage causes us to feel some sense of choice and/or control coming back into our lives as we make powerful decisions about how we will move forward and rebuild our lives.

7. **Acceptance:** As we step into the final stage of the grieving process, BetterHelp.com says, "Accepting a loss does

not mean that you simply 'get over it' or are content with what happened. Rather, it is the part of the process during which you can acknowledge the loss and feel okay with moving forward with your life and what the new normal is for you."[3] In this stage, you'll still experience memories of loss—but these memories will no longer bring you to your knees in deep anguish like they used to. You'll begin to breathe again and find hope, likely with a new willingness to openly talk about the loss, even if there is sadness or regret attached to it. You'll come to a place of acceptance and be able to talk about your personal story without shame, desiring to carve out new memories, allowing the grief to shape and mature you, proud that you've moved through it.

TEARS, SHAKE SHACK, AND SALT LAKE CITY

We'd lived in Charleston, South Carolina, for just under seven months when I went on a trip to Sacramento for a speaking engagement. I was on a layover in Salt Lake City, eating Shake Shack, when I realized that I hadn't let myself really miss or grieve New York after twelve years of life there. I had already faced the shock and denial, pain and guilt, and anger and bargaining, but a moment of reflection presented itself, and I found myself openly moving through another stage of the grieving process.

Truthfully, I thought we would've been in New York City into retirement, surrounded by our children and grandchildren at boisterous Thanksgiving and Christmas gatherings in our Brooklyn apartment. Well, let me tell you, that delicious burger brought back old memories of sitting in Madison Square Park, eating Shake Shack for the very first time. I remembered that with each bite I'd found my love deepening for the city we'd been called to. I loved our assignment in New York, on the best and worst of days. It was sure and clear. I remember being aware of the feelings in my body as I sat in Salt Lake and ate those crinkle-cut fries, and the overwhelming memories actually stunned me. I'm usually pretty unafraid of facing my stuff, but something just under the surface started to come up for me. By experiencing so much compounded pain pastoring in New York through 2020 and 2021, I had unintentionally lumped our twelve years in the city all together, viewing them through the lens of our last two years there, forgetting about all the good. I had been letting the depths of discouragement narrate the story I told myself over and over again, staining a period of time that was actually God-breathed in the first place and filled with different degrees of hope, joy, tragedy, pain, and everything in between.

I realized the transition into our new life in South Carolina had been surprisingly beautiful, filled with peace, ease, and a sense of belonging. We'd made such good friends in such a short amount of time, and the church we'd become a part of welcomed us with wide-open arms. We'd found such healing; our kids were flourishing and so was our marriage. I hadn't purposefully been avoiding grieving our move from New York; I'd just been swept up in gratitude for the new season we were in.

I'd gotten to this revelatory moment through a series of delays that turned a six-hour travel day into a twelve-hour travel day. On the flight from Salt Lake to Sacramento, I decided to go through my phone and delete screenshots and old videos that were irrelevant and taking up space in the cloud. While I reviewed eleven years' worth of memories, many of them brought me to tears as I realized my kids' lives were flashing before my eyes. I reminisced about the days of going to our neighborhood park, Central Park, grabbing our favorite bagel or slice of greasy pepperoni pizza, walking the mile to Trader Joe's and back while the kids were little, spending time with friends, enjoying the crisp fall air, Fifth Avenue in December, the first snow of the season turning the city into a magical movie set, worshiping with our people, and so much more. These were good memories—core, meaningful memories. There were other pictures I'd pondered deleting because they had people in them who had disappeared from our lives as though Thanos from *Avengers: Infinity War* had snapped his fingers (yes, this is a spoiler) and half the population vanished.

Instead of isolating myself and diving into a sad spiral, I decided to text my husband and a couple of friends and ask them to pray for me because I'd become the embarrassing crier on the plane, and the flood of awkward tears was showing no signs of stopping. You know those "the dam burst" moments, where there is no holding back the flood that's coming forth? Yeah, that's what was happening to me. Thank goodness I was beside a window so I could turn and pretend I was looking outside, and the view was so beautiful that I couldn't stop crying.

One of my friends responded:

> Praying for you this morning! Give yourself some space and permission to grieve! No one likes to grieve, but as Dr. Anita said, there's no bad emotion—it's temporary. Don't run from it—just allow yourself and your kids to walk through it. Healthy grieving is just that—healthy. You left an entire life—with people and friends and a church you love and were assigned to. The excitement and joy of the new has distracted you from the grief and now you are settled and beginning to feel. And that's ok! Believing our God will hold you with such tenderness like his precious child. Loved beyond measure. Love you friend.

I needed to let God hold me. His Word came flooding back to me . . . *He comforts those who mourn.*

Here's a seemingly simple question: Have you given yourself permission and space to grieve? You may say or think things like "Everyone needs me," "I don't want to be seen as weak," "I have too much to do," or "I'm not the crying type." Saying or thinking like this will stunt our personal and spiritual growth. If we don't give ourselves permission to grieve, we don't give ourselves permission to grow.

Remember, grief is a gift whether it hits you while you're in Salt Lake City, outside a bagel shop, driving in your car, in the shower, at the movies, sitting with a friend, or lying in your bed at night. Let it flow. Let the Comforter comfort you.

A BIBLICAL LOOK AT GRIEF

If you're not convinced yet that grief can cause us to grow and heal, let's look at it from a biblical perspective, starting with Jesus. Not only did He grieve, but He bore all of our grief. The prophet Isaiah foretold it in Isaiah 53.

> Surely he took up our pain
> and bore our suffering. (v. 4)

He was also fully God and fully human. He walked a mile in our shoes when it came to experiencing loss, pain, and grief. He felt things deeply. Remember when Jesus publicly wept at Lazarus's tomb in John 11:35? Or the funeral procession in Luke 7:12–13, where Jesus's "heart went out" to a widow in grief who had lost her only son, "and he said, 'Don't cry'"? What about when He wept as He approached Jerusalem, aching for His people to repent and turn to Him, as He prophetically saw the coming destruction of the Holy City after His resurrection (Luke 19:41–44)? Or when He was overwhelmed with grief and fear in the garden of

Gethsemane: "Then Jesus came with them to a place called Gethsemane, and told His disciples, 'Sit here while I go over there and
pray.' And He took Peter and the two sons of Zebedee with Him,
and began to be grieved and distressed. Then He said to them,
'My soul is deeply grieved, to the point of death; remain here and
keep watch with Me'" (Matt. 26:36–38 NASB). Jesus shows us that
grief is part of the human experience.

The Psalms are powerful passages of Scripture to read out loud
as prayers in times of grief. Take Psalm 6, for example, written by
David as a prayer for those suffering through sickness, distress,
pain, or oppression:

> O LORD, don't rebuke me in your anger
>   or discipline me in your rage.
> Have compassion on me, LORD, for I am weak.
>   Heal me, LORD, for my bones are in agony.
> I am sick at heart.
>   How long, O LORD, until you restore me?
>
> Return, O LORD, and rescue me.
>   Save me because of your unfailing love.
> For the dead do not remember you.
>   Who can praise you from the grave?
>
> *I am worn out from sobbing.*
>   *All night I flood my bed with weeping,*
>   *drenching it with my tears.*
> *My vision is blurred by grief;*
>   my eyes are worn out because of all my enemies.
>
> Go away, all you who do evil,
>   for the LORD has heard my weeping.
> The LORD has heard my plea;
>   the LORD will answer my prayer.
> May all my enemies be disgraced and terrified.
>   May they suddenly turn back in shame. (NLT)

What about Lamentations? The book we misunderstand or rarely read unless we're going through the *One Year Bible*? In an article for the BibleProject, Whitney Woollard writes,

> Lamentations isn't a "feel-good" book. Actually, it's a total downer. It's a collection of five lament or "funeral" poems (poems of sorrow and mourning) that give voice to the grief of God's people in the wake of Jerusalem's fall and Judah's demise in 587 BC. The book mourns the day, warned of by the prophets, when God became like an enemy to Israel, giving them over to Babylon because of their chronic disregard for his covenant. . . . Lamentations gives you the emotions, emotions that are raw, honest, dark, and even volatile at times. That's why this is the book of grief in the Bible.[4]

I know from experience, and I'm sure you do too, just how tender and raw those emotions can get. Maybe consider reading and understanding Lamentations in a new way, allowing it to cause you to embrace your pain with the Healer instead of running from or avoiding it.

One night, in a personal season of lament, I couldn't sleep and I felt a nudge from the Holy Spirit to put my earbuds in and listen to the book of Job. Not the most comforting book but one of loss, despair, and redemption. Peace descended, and the tension in my body and my inability to find rest ceased. Sometimes we need to go to uncomfortable places, just as those who have gone before us have, to find rest for our weary souls in the midst of the tempests that grief can bring.

Remember that storms are promised in Matthew 7, and what we've built our lives on before those storms hit is up to us. We desperately need a biblical foundation when it comes to weathering the torrents of grief, pain, betrayal, and loss. At times we find ourselves in liminal spaces, with one foot in what was and the other in what will be. And it aches, but our faith journey is filled with moments like these. We as the church have not always been good at being present to help people move through the complex recovery journey of grief and loss—because it will cost us to come alongside someone else's pain. I think we may have collectively believed the lie that if we don't walk in faith and faith alone in a painful season or situation, then we are somehow faithless, which simply isn't true.

The Shunammite woman in 2 Kings 4 shows us that walking in the tension of faith and brutal honesty is taking the necessary pathway to restoration. She was a well-to-do woman living in Shunem, whose house the prophet Elisha would frequent for a good meal. She and her husband end up building a room on the roof for the prophet to stay in when he passes through town. In his gratitude he asks what can be done for her, and her response is, in essence, "All is well; we want for nothing." But Gehazi, the prophet's servant, points out the painfully obvious reality that she is barren, and she and her husband are old. Elisha prophesies that at the same time the following year, she'll embrace a son. Her reaction isn't one of joy, though; instead, she says, "No, my lord, O man of God; do not lie to your servant" (v. 16 ESV).

Culturally and personally, she had already suffered so much loss and public disgrace by being barren into her old age that she didn't want her hopes raised. Yet in the end, the prophet's word comes to pass and she holds a son in her arms. But years later, in a brutal plot twist, the miracle goes sideways as her son also dies in those same loving arms. I can only imagine the emotions that would have rippled out of her in those moments of disbelief and despair. The woman lays her dead son on the bed of the man of God, shuts the door, and then does everything in her power to get to the man of God as quickly as possible. When she gets there, Elisha sees her in the distance and tells Gehazi,

"Run at once to meet her and say to her, 'Is all well with you? Is all well with your husband? Is all well with the child?'" And she answered, "All is well." And when she came to the mountain to the man of God, she caught hold of his feet. And Gehazi came to push her away. But the man of God said, "Leave her alone, for she is in bitter distress, and the LORD has hidden it from me and has not told me." Then she said, *"Did I ask my lord for a son? Did I not say, 'Do not deceive me?'"* (vv. 26–28 ESV)

Up until that moment, she's acted in faith, putting her son on the bed of the man of God, telling her husband all is well when it clearly isn't, saddling a donkey, and riding seventeen to eighteen miles to get to the man of God quickly. And when she gets there, she doesn't want to talk to Gehazi; she wants to talk to the prophet, the one who'd said she'd hold a son in her arms. And she isn't sweet with her words. Instead, she's brutally honest in her grief. She walks in the tension of faith and honesty, and she cries out to the man of God to petition God on her behalf.

The story ends in resurrection. The man of God is so moved that he follows her back to her house and raises her son from the dead. But what about the times when this is not our story? When loss feels like it may just swallow us whole? When the tears feel like they'll never stop soaking our pillow? When the tangible ache in our heart seems to never end?

Walking in the tension of heartache and hope all at once is like riding on a roller coaster we didn't willingly line up to get on. Somehow we've believed the lie that if we lament, we're simply broken, but as we can see, it's the biblical and human journey toward healing. You can be ravaged with tears at the loss of a loved one and at the same time find yourself enjoying your job, your relationships, and the good work you put your hand to, recognizing that deep within, it is truly well with your soul.

GIVE YOURSELF PERMISSION TO GRIEVE AND CHANGE

The discomfort with grief is that life goes on. The clock keeps ticking forward, people forget to check in, we still need to get out of bed to go to work or care for our loved ones . . . people change, and so do we. Things simply cannot remain as they were—there's no going back.

Remember the quote that opened this chapter? "Grieving is a necessary passage and a difficult transition to finally letting go of sorrow—it is not a permanent rest stop."

As we begin to wrap up this chapter, can I encourage you to give yourself permission and space to grieve? There is no perfect formula for this because you are so wildly unique and so is your human experience. If you need an intentional retreat, plan it, book it, and commit to it. If you need to warn your family not to come into your bedroom for the next hour or so because it's going to get ugly in there, let them know, and then lock the door and let the grief out. Put on that song that holds memories so deep in your bones, you can't help but let the floodgates open. Your tears are healing. If you need someone to pray with you, sit with you, or listen to you, be bold and ask for what you need—you are worthy of love and someone else's time. If you need a counselor or prayer, do whatever it takes to find someone you can trust, and then show up, even if you're nervous to face what you need to face. If you need to stop being the workhorse and pretending that your achievements or your busybody, nonstop doing of all the things is somehow healing something in you, start to let go of control— on purpose. If depression and anxiety are like wet blankets that weigh you down and threaten to pull you, with your greasy, matted, unwashed hair, back into bed for another day, have a game plan to swing those feet over the side of the bed no matter how you feel. Get in the shower, go on a walk, exercise, read a dramatic, soul-wrenching psalm out loud, call a friend when you don't feel like it—whatever it takes to move through it—simply do it, even when it seems like the absolute hardest thing to do. It's true, you may fall apart as you acknowledge that your heart is shattered into a thousand little pieces, but remember that through it all, God's *really* good at putting things back together in a much better way than we ever could've asked or imagined Him to.

Give yourself permission to release the past and change. After seismic life events, we have to accept that we'll simply never be the same, nor will those around us, *which means* you have permission to change. Let go of the identity you formed to pacify and satisfy the expectations of others. They may not understand as you move on, but let go of the need to please others and stay grounded in and centered on Jesus, braving change and the grief that comes with it.

BUILDING ON THE ROCK

Scripture Meditation: Matthew 5:4

> Blessed are those who mourn,
> for they will be comforted.

In context, this verse comes at the start of the Sermon on the Mount, the very sermon that ends with one of our key Scriptures in this book, Matthew 7:24–27, which starts, "Therefore everyone who hears these words of mine and puts them into practice is like a wise man who built his house on the rock." With that in mind as you meditate on Matthew 5:4, how can you put it into practice and build your life on the Rock, even in the midst of pain?

REFLECTION QUESTIONS

- If you're going through a major loss, where are you in the seven stages of grief? Where do you need to be gentle with yourself?
- Where do you need to give yourself permission to grieve, and how will you go about it as you remember that God comforts those who mourn?

GUIDED PRAYER

Father, I feel so many emotions, it's hard to pinpoint where to even begin. As David prayed in Psalm 6, "I am worn out from sobbing. All night I flood my bed with weeping, drenching it with my tears. My vision is blurred by grief . . ." I need You, God. My walls have been broken down. I can no longer fix the problems around me, and I can't go back in time. I am at the end of my rope, and I need You to heal my shattered heart. Forgive me for not letting You in, for not allowing You to comfort me. Guide me in my brokenness and hold me with Your righteous and tender hand. I trust You to heal me and make me whole again, even when I do not have the answers to all of my why questions. I am safe within Your arms, and in that, it is well with my soul.

CHAPTER 4

A TIME TO RECOVER

I have come so that they may have life and have it in abundance.

Jesus, in John 10:10 (CSB)

"Please never call me resilient again; I just need some time to heal and recover." These were the words out of the mouth of a good friend who at the time had recently experienced a series of major losses back-to-back. We'd been looking at memes at the time and couldn't stop laugh-crying because of their brutal honesty, including one with the theme of resilience, which had gotten us really good. Fun fact: My editor told me that books with the word *resilient* in the title or subtitle don't usually sell as well (unless you're an established *New York Times* bestseller). Who knew? (My publisher did, that's who.) Maybe it's our subconscious stubbornness when we're at an all-time low that instinctively knows we need something else besides a pat on the back for being "resilient" when it feels like it's all going to hell in a handbasket. Sometimes we just need a good nap.

We don't get a gold star for pushing ahead, pretending like all is well when the best thing for us could be taking a moment to recover from the losses we've suffered. Grief is real, but so is the journey to recovery and restoration. Yes, we *will* talk about endurance and perseverance (also known as resilience) because James 1 and Hebrews 12 (and many other Scriptures) are very clear about these things.

Before we dive in any further to this chapter, let me explain what I mean when I say "recovery" or "a time to recover." This is twofold: you will need a game plan to heal from the change and/or loss (recovery), and you may need to set aside a time or season to do so (a time to recover). The goal is not to get stuck and stay in recovery mode but to move forward because our God is a redemptive and restorative God. As my friend Irene says, "If we're not working on our recovery, we're working on our relapse." In other words, if we're not in forward motion partnering with God, doing the work of daily disciplines, we're stagnant or going backward. So, what does *recover*, or *recovery*, mean?

Recover

1. Return to a normal state of health, mind, or strength.
2. Find or regain possession of (something stolen or lost).[1]

John 10:10 reminds us that the thief comes only to steal, kill, and destroy our lives, but Christ has come to give us life and life to the full. In other words, in every way that the enemy has tried to destroy your life, Jesus has come to recover the losses, to make all things new and give you an abundant life. If you look at the context of John 10, Jesus is telling those listening (including the Pharisees at the time) that *He* is the Good Shepherd. He breaks down what it looks like to follow Him and move at the sound of His voice alone. He says that His followers will know the sound of His voice, the voice that leads us home to safety and healing.

Let's look at several different translations of John 10:10. As you read each one, what do you see? What pattern stands out to you? What does it show you about Jesus?

CSB

A thief comes only to steal and kill and destroy. I have come so that they may have life and have it in abundance.

ESV

The thief comes only to steal and kill and destroy. I came that they may have life and have it abundantly.

KJV

The thief cometh not, but for to steal, and to kill, and to destroy: I am come that they might have life, and that they might have it more abundantly.

MSG

A thief is only there to steal and kill and destroy. I came so they can have real and eternal life, more and better life than they ever dreamed of.

NLT

The thief's purpose is to steal and kill and destroy. My purpose is to give them a rich and satisfying life.

The thief's purpose is clear: He steals from us with an expectation that we'll lie down and take it. He has a literal plan to kill us and derail us from our destinies, to silence us in our callings and bring the ultimate destruction of our lives, our family lines, and the generations to come. He only has death to give versus Jesus, who doesn't take from us but willingly laid down His life to give us life "abundantly," "a rich and satisfying life," "real and eternal life,"

life "in abundance." There is a clear dichotomy here. If you have been stolen from, assaulted with a spirit of death at any point, or felt like your life was being shattered and destroyed, whether by your own choices or the choices of others, there is an appropriate time to recognize, acknowledge, and grieve what has happened, and then there is a time to heal. We teach the enemy how he can speak to us by what we continue to allow. We have to relearn what it is not to leave the front door of our spiritual lives open to demonic destruction, and we have to allow Jesus, the Good Shepherd, to show us *how* to recover and live life intentionally wrapped in Him and His abundance.

SPIRIT, SOUL, AND BODY

In the healing process, it's important to remember that we're spirit, soul, and body. You may be thinking, *I know, I know*, but stay with me. We're triune beings created in the image of a triune God, who is three in one: Father, Son, and Holy Spirit. Depending on our upbringing within the church, or completely outside of the church, we're all going to have a natural leaning and/or lens toward what feels comfortable for us when it comes to recovery, restoration, and healing.

If you grew up in Pentecostal or charismatic circles, I can almost guarantee that you're very familiar with deliverance and that you're down to command any demon that shows itself to leave in the name of Jesus. You're probably also familiar with practices that center you on Jesus as Healer, cultivating the presence of God, and reading the Word daily, as well as regular discipleship. Being aware of and attuned to the spiritual realm is a strength.

Others of you may have grown up in a more traditional church with more practical, methodical approaches to healing, like Celebrate Recovery, GriefShare, or AA groups, intentional regular discipleship, strong teaching in the Word that propels you to personally be in the Word, and/or going to therapy without shame. These are avenues that help heal with the *mind, will, and emotions*—our *soul*. Yes, there is spirit and soul crossover but possibly with a partial leaning.

And others of you who may or may not have grown up in church at all are aware of the spiritual realm, know that care of the soul matters, and also are aware that taking care of our physical *bodies*—eating well, exercising, getting enough sleep, and generally staying active—is good for our well-being and an obvious path to recovery after a major life change or loss. Our bodies are the actual temple of the Holy Spirit, so keeping a clean, fit, and healthy house is paramount to our recovery journey.

I find, in times of major change, we need to be mindful of our rhythms in our spiritual walk, including how we're attending to our body and soul. Every single part of who we are created to be needs our intentionality and care to walk in all that Christ died and rose again to give us. Below is a simple diagram to show you how our spirit, soul, and body overlap. As a note, your spirit is God-conscious, your soul is self-conscious, and your body is world-conscious.

As someone who is passionate about wholeness in Christ, I cannot stress enough how much we have to pay attention to all three of these parts of our life. I am not ashamed to say that I have been delivered from demons and am so grateful for freedom in Christ. I love to read the Word of God daily, wake early to pray, and practice the presence of God with daily gratitude, repentance, forgiveness, worship, and communion. I have also done the work as a recovering codependent in Celebrate Recovery with a group of pastors, sat in therapy with a licensed Christian counselor (and will continue to whenever the need arises) to create new neural pathways and be transformed by the renewal of my mind, and engaged in intentional discipleship with my peers. I will continue to choose to make healing choices centered on Christ, allowing my God-given emotions to be indicators of what is going on at a deeper level. I continue to take care of my body as it ages because it is a temple.

SO, WHAT'S YOUR GAME PLAN?

PTSD, panic attacks, angry outbursts, demonic heaviness as I slept, and suspicions ran my life through 2020 and the beginning of 2021. In Celebrate Recovery language, "my hurts, hang-ups, and habits" had the reins of my life, and I wasn't sure how to get them back—so I phoned a friend. Irene Rollins was that friend.

Talking to her brought hope back into my soul. I shook as I dialed her number, but the more I let the darkness out, the lighter I felt and the less I shook. I told her things that only a very small circle of people know about me. Irene has often said, "Be authentic with the many and vulnerable with a few," meaning show up as your true self wherever you go, don't play games, and don't pander to the crowd or cultural norms—be you. Walk in healing and know who you are. *But also*—not everyone gets to have our heart or walk through the process with us. That's why writing vulnerable posts on social media without being in a place of overcoming can be so unhealthy. We give a virtual community—who is not going to show up for us in human form, hang out in our mundane, or celebrate us in our greatest achievements—a place to comment and counsel us in our most vulnerable hour. Who cheers you on, sits with you in and through every season, is with you at your lowest, doesn't leave, and when you're successful is not intimidated by you and doesn't want something from you? Those are your people.

All that aside, after I poured out my heart, Irene honored my vulnerability, thanked me for sharing with her, and then said, "Well, you're going to be okay, *and* we need a game plan." She proceeded to counsel me on next steps, and for me that was a two-week counseling intensive at a Christian counseling center in the United States, which included EMDR sessions.[2] She also opened up a virtual Celebrate Recovery Step Study group for pastors only and asked me to be a part of it for weekly support and accountability. Celebrate Recovery isn't just for addiction; it's also for recovery from physical, sexual, and emotional abuse; food and body-image issues; codependency; and so much more.[3] This group has deeply changed my life. It's intentional discipleship for those on a journey of healing.

I continued to regularly go to church, even when I wanted to stay in bed with the covers wrapped safely around me, hiding me from the world. I got up, got dressed, gathered my family, and chose to worship God when I wanted to hide and make life all about me. I checked in with and opened up to Irene and my CR (Celebrate Recovery) group, not allowing anything to remain hidden that could potentially be damaging to me or others around me. I've learned that when the enemy tries to gain a foothold in my life, I purposefully slam the door on that foot.

So, what's *your* game plan? What's one thing you can start today, or plan in the coming weeks or months, that will bring lasting change?

- Maybe it's time to book a retreat at a hotel or retreat center to rest, reflect, and pray for twenty-four to forty-eight hours. Take some time to get away from the noise and ask Jesus for a game plan.

- It's possible that you need to confess or repent of some things to your spouse or a trusted friend. Maybe you need to walk through a forgiveness prayer for a few people or take some time to repent of things that have been damaging to your life. There's no better time than the present. Who do you need to call and open up your life to right after you finish reading this?

- Who are one or two people you can really trust and *choose* to be accountable with regularly? And as a side note, please don't make them poke and prod you to get the truth out of you. We need to understand that we'll be as accountable as we want to be. No one can force us to open up and be vulnerable—it's a powerful choice we can make to bring lasting change.

- Maybe it's time to understand and/or do some training in deliverance ministry.⁴ Jesus regularly cast out demons, so understanding this is incredibly important in our faith journey.

- Look up Celebrate Recovery, GriefShare, or Christian counselors in your area and commit to doing the weekly work. Make an appointment or send an email today—get the ball rolling. Immediate obedience to the nudge of the Holy Spirit changes things.

- Choose to get into a Bible study, discipleship group, or small group in your church. Weekly commitments to engage in fellowship paired with a desire to become more like Christ *in* community bring higher levels of accountability into your life. If you don't show up, it matters because you have chosen to allow yourself to be known, and when you're not there, you're missed.

- I can't stress enough not to neglect gathering together, as some are in the habit of doing, to worship God with the saints and minister to one another weekly. Even when you don't feel like it. Hebrews 10:23–25 says, "Let us hold unswervingly to the hope we profess, for he who promised is faithful. And let us consider how we may spur one another on toward love and good deeds, not giving up meeting together, as some are in the habit of doing, but encouraging one another—and all the more as you see the Day approaching."

- What do you need to do to get healthier physically? If you don't work out, what's one thing you can commit to doing that will get your body moving? Even just beginning to walk out in nature or the streets of your neighborhood three times a week is a good start. You know your body; you know what you need—where can you begin?

- What's one thing you can change about how you eat today? Cut out sugar? Eat more greens? Throw out the garbage you have in your pantry? What's a sustainable plan you can live by and not a fad that will fade away?

One day, one choice, one step at a time. A surrendered life built on the Rock, along with a good game plan, can help us withstand the storms and major changes of life.

A HELPFUL TOOL

I'm about to share a tool to take with you on the journey as you navigate change, loss, transition, and new seasons. This tool can be used within your game plan to keep you healthy and grounded in Christ.

When I went to my counseling intensive, one of the key things I learned was the following progression to identify the root of my pain so that I could heal and recover quickly instead of circling the mountain of my hurts, hang-ups, and habits:

WOUNDS → LIES → FALSE BELIEFS → STRONGHOLDS → VOWS → FALSE SELF

Wounds

Wounds can come from anyone, anywhere, at any time. Whether you have a fresh wound from today or are still ruminating (in the back of your mind) over a wound that took place when you were a three-year-old, they will continue to affect you if you don't purposefully identify and root them out. We have to understand that Jesus has come to redeem and restore all things, to see His Kingdom come and His will be done here on earth as it is in heaven. But we still live in the great in-between, the now but not yet. Jesus has come to emancipate us from our sin and give us eternal life, but He has not yet returned for His bride, and we do not live within a new heaven and earth. Therefore, we have to remember that we have an enemy who prowls around like a roaring lion, seeking whom he may devour—his time is short, and he's on a mission to steal, kill, and destroy. Our wounds usually come through another wounded person whether they intend to hurt us or not. If you can, try to see the spiritual side of your pain instead of targeting the person it came through. And remember, the enemy of our soul is hell-bent on keeping us wounded, offended, bitter, and unforgiving.

86

When we identify a wound, we initiate the healing process *if* we don't remain meditating on the uncovered wound(s). The next step is identifying the lie.

Lies

The moment a wounding takes place, Satan loves to plant a lie that will germinate and grow, becoming a false belief system that we begin to live by. If we can identify the lies we've believed that are connected to a specific wound, we are then empowered to begin to replace it with the truth! This is paramount to our healing and restoration journey.

False Beliefs

False belief systems are directly connected to the lies that we believe, hold on to, and allow to take root in our lives. They become a lens through which we view relationships, the church, our cities, different people groups, and even how we interpret the Word of God.

Once you begin to identify false belief systems, you will be blown away at how getting a fresh lens changes how you view the world. Once you've identified them, ask God to give you *true* belief systems to replace the false ones. Every time you begin to see yourself going down the negative roads you used to, stop yourself, repent, and ask Jesus to show you how to see clearly and correctly.

Strongholds

Strongholds are our self-protection mechanisms, birthed out of a false belief system (rooted in a lie), that alert us that we're not safe out in this big, bad, chaotic world. So, we have to find ways to protect ourselves against attack instead of letting God protect and defend us.

Stronghold can be defined as

1. a place that has been fortified so as to protect it against attack.
2. a place where a particular cause or belief is strongly defended or upheld.[5]

What's your shield or stronghold of choice? Anger; rage; isolation; fight, flight, fawn, or freeze; control; manipulation; avoidance; cynicism; blame; slander; gossip; suspicion . . . This list can be long and personal here. The good news is that what is revealed can be healed.

Once we identify what we self-protect with, we have to be proactive to repent daily and do something different. True repentance comes out of a heart that is genuinely broken by our actions and past conduct and how they've affected us, the ones we love, and our relationship with God. It's followed by a dedication to live differently and purposefully make different choices.

The safest place we can run is into the arms of a loving God. Listen, it's true; it's not always safe out there and people will hurt us again, but I'd rather have my Rock, my Fortress, my Deliverer, Shield, and Stronghold do what He does best. Sometimes we need to lay down our sword so that we can run into the shelter of the Most High God.

> The LORD is my rock, my fortress and my deliverer;
> my God is my rock, in whom I take refuge,
> my shield and the horn of my salvation, my stronghold.
> (Ps. 18:2)

Vows

In its simplest form, a vow is a promise to do a specific thing. There are healthy and unhealthy vows.

Vows to your spouse on your wedding day are common healthy vows. But here are a few examples of unhealthy vows:

- I will never trust the church again.
- I will always be like this.
- I will never trust another man again.
- I will never trust another woman again.
- I will never trust _____ again.
- I will always be alone.
- I won't ever be fully healed and whole.
- I will never forgive _____.
- I will prove that they were wrong about me.
- I will never let them take anything from me.
- I will never be hurt again.
- Write your own:

_____

_____

_____

Often, we declare these vows "safe" within our stronghold of self-protection. When these vows become stronger than our vow to lay down our lives, follow Jesus, and live within the goodness of the gospel, it's time to *renounce* some unhealthy vows that have held us bound. Here is a prayer you can pray to do so:

Father, I come before You to willingly renounce the vows that I thought would protect me from further pain or harm. I've realized that I'm only hurting myself, and I ask for Your forgiveness for walking in self-protection while declaring these unhealthy vows. These vows have only led to further fear, distrust, and suspicion in my life, and I desperately want to trust You with all that I am. Right now, I renounce these vow(s): [Confess all vows here]. In the name of Jesus, I break the power that these vows have held over my life, and I repent of my sin of not trusting You. I lean into Your mercy, grace, love, and justice and trust that You uphold me with Your righteous hand. Help me not to fall back into these vows by the power of Your Holy Spirit convicting me and leading me into all truth. I ask that You bring healing and renewal in my life and in relationships that have been damaged or affected by these vows. I receive Your grace and mercy in Jesus's name, amen.

False Self

When we unknowingly live life with unidentified wounds, lies, false beliefs, strongholds, and vows, it's hard to be sure of who we are.

Now, I know our "true self" is consistently transforming and hard to grasp as we follow Jesus and become more like Him in our journey of sanctification, but that's kind of the point! We're works in progress, disciples of Christ, walking in healing and restoration as He puts the broken things back together in the deeply redemptive way that only He can. We start to walk a bit more confidently in who we are wrapped up in Christ. We don't long for others to tell us because we're doing the work to uncover the truth ourselves. We may walk with a limp as we figure things out and use this tool (daily if we need to), but we'll be able to move forward authentically.

A FINAL NOTE: WHY WE NEED A GAME PLAN TO RECOVER

In case you're not quite convinced you need a game plan for recovery, let me just share one last thing with you.

In days gone by, I preached a message that can be found online called "Get Out of the Boat," based off Peter, his denial of Christ, and his restoration. Peter's passion is grandiose, and he's so deeply human. His zeal to follow Jesus with everything is palpable, and his denial is just as visceral. I love the progression of Peter's journey, his struggle, and his willingness to get back up again after failure. Jesus's restoration of Peter after His resurrection is so intimate.

I remember reading the Gospel of John and the following words from chapter 21 jumping off the page. This is after Peter's denial, Jesus's resurrection, and even Jesus's appearance to the disciples:

> Afterward Jesus appeared again to his disciples, by the Sea of Galilee. It happened this way: Simon Peter, Thomas (also known as Didymus), Nathanael from Cana in Galilee, the sons of Zebedee, and two other disciples were together. *"I'm going out to fish,"* Simon Peter told them, and they said, *"We'll go with you."* So they went out and got into the boat, *but that night they caught nothing.* (vv. 1–3)

Peter had seen the risen Messiah, even shared a room with Him (imagine the conviction you'd feel making eye contact after denying Him!), and didn't fall on his knees in repentance asking for forgiveness. No—instead, he went back to what was familiar, his life of fishing, and notice, he didn't go alone. Some of the other disciples came with him, *and* it was fruitless! They caught nothing!

When we don't do the work of healing and recovery, repentance and renewal, we go back to what is familiar. Like Peter, we often don't go alone—others are watching and following us—and it's fruitless because our true restoration is in Jesus! We will continue to go back to what is familiar after failure because we haven't chosen to jump out of the boat, eat breakfast with Jesus, and allow Him to restore us like only He can. (Read the whole of John 21.) Peter could've stayed in the boat, ashamed of his choices, and been embarrassed for catching nothing in his efforts to fish, the only trade he ever knew before he left everything to follow the Rabbi. But he humbled himself, took off his outer garment, ran to shore, and let Jesus speak the truth in love to him.

Two of my favorite passages in the book of Acts say, "In those days *Peter stood up* among the brother and sisters" (1:15 CSB) and "*Peter stood up* with the Eleven, raised his voice, and proclaimed to them . . ." (2:14 CSB). The only thing that gave Peter the dignity to *stand up* and lead after public denial and failure was the restoring power of Jesus. Peter stood up and led the charge in choosing Matthias, the new apostle, to replace Judas. And he also preached the first sermon after Pentecost, calling thousands to repentance, seeing "about three thousand" repent, be baptized, and be added to the number of saints (2:41). Imagine he didn't get out of that boat. Imagine he didn't unashamedly run to Jesus. Imagine he didn't allow himself to be corrected, loved, and restored. But he did. And then he *stood up*—and so can you.

I can't encourage you enough—get a game plan, bring in people you trust, do the work, and allow Jesus to do what only He can do. I'll say Irene's words one more time: "If we're not working on our recovery, we're working on our relapse." Peter shows us this, but he also shows us how to humble ourselves and stand up again.

BUILDING ON THE ROCK

Scripture Meditation: Psalm 18:2

> The LORD is my rock, my fortress and my deliverer;
>> my God is my rock, in whom I take refuge,
>> my shield and the horn of my salvation, my stronghold.

As you ponder and meditate on this Scripture, what names of God are true for you? Is He your rock? Your fortress? Deliverer? Shield and horn of your salvation? Your stronghold? And in what areas do you step in and self-protect rather than running to God?

Take a moment and read this passage out loud, and then thank Him for who He is in your life.

REFLECTION QUESTIONS

- What is the first action step you're going to take in initiating your "game plan"?
- Who are you going to reach out to today to get the ball rolling and choose accountability in this process? Remember, we're as accountable as we want to be.

GUIDED PRAYER

Lord, I thank You for the cross and the resurrection of Jesus Christ more than ever. Your grace and mercy to save, heal, and deliver me are beyond my wildest imagination, and I am so grateful at how far You go to rescue and redeem my life. Forgive me for all the times I have run away, hidden, or walked in unforgiveness, denial, offense, or bitterness—these roadblocks have kept me from humbling myself and running to You. Holy Spirit, speak to me and show me the way. Lovingly correct me and remind me of all truth. Please light the path to a God-given game plan to walk in restoration and healing in Christ. I trust You.

CHAPTER 5

LEARNING FROM CHANGE

Change is the end result of all true learning.

Leo Buscaglia

Ideally, we never stop learning, which means we never stop growing.

I've recognized in my own life that we can either learn from what we've gone through or take the same test over and over again with each new season.

On September 29, 2020, I posted this prophetic word on Instagram. I had sat on it for almost a year after God had given it to me, unsure as to whether it was for me to share or simply intercede over. In the end, it was both/and:

At the end of 2019, we had a flood in our basement. Literally, the day after Christmas gift to yours truly was a flood. We didn't know if it was sewage water from a burst pipe or city water. We were hoping for the latter.

Our landlord and a team of people worked around the clock to fix the problem. They drilled a hole in the foundation to find the pipe, to test the water, to fix the pipe, to . . . you get the picture. It was a mess. Workers came and went at all hours because we couldn't have this leak in the foundation of our house, and we needed to know if it was sewage. (It wasn't, by the way.)

I heard the Lord say, "I am fixing the cracks and leaks in the foundation of the church."

Well, I thought he just meant Liberty Church (which He is 100% doing that), but it's clear now He is reforming and renewing His entire bride—the church—through this crushing and pressing moment we find ourselves in on planet earth. And He's starting with yours truly. He is exposing cracks and leaks in the foundation and bringing solutions with (I believe) those who are willing to do the work and walk out the process. It can be confusing, messy, and require some long-suffering. And goodness, I'm so aware that criticism (of self or others) won't build anything. I mean, remember Sanballat and Tobiah criticizing Nehemiah for rebuilding a broken wall? Yeah, we have to choose not to be them. I want to be a part of the solution, picking up charred and broken stones while asking God what and where to rebuild.

May we bring it back to the simple things (because there is no magic pill)—being disciples of Jesus who follow in His way, His truth, and His life that make other disciples. So, if we need to, let's repent of living in our own way, our own truth, and our own life (I do daily). If God has been exposing the leaks and cracks in your foundation, it's because He loves you. Will we submit to His will or our own? My goodness, He's such a loving Father.

I believe we are on the brink of something truly magnificent and it will take our individual and collective effort to live as followers of the Way to see renewal in our cities. Like Jesus, let's do what we see the Father doing.

Why share this prophetic word? Well, I sincerely hope and pray that we as the church across the earth didn't just survive 2020–2021 but that it changed us for the better, even if we're hobbling a bit, bearing scars that testify to God's faithfulness and healing. That we allowed God to fix the cracks in the foundation of the church (i.e., our lives, because we are the church). That we learned new things, grew our roots down deep, repented of pride and sin, walked in wisdom, and followed in the way of Jesus with radical obedience, reverence, and awe. That we made amends wherever helpful and possible. That we stood up again, remembering what truly matters in life. That we absorbed all that God had for us in the shaking, pruning, and cutting off.

It's good (and hard) to remember that God disciplines those He loves. It's what a good father does. Lawless children are a thorn in the flesh of their parents. Discipline is integral in teaching our children to own their mistakes and walk in the consequences of their choices in hopes that next time they'll humbly do things differently. It's also the hope that they'll get to a place of personal conviction to willingly make amends with their siblings or elders. When we as parents constantly own or cover up our kids' foolish choices or interfere to save them from themselves, they'll never learn the pain of regret, which leads to godly sorrow and true repentance. Instead, they'll only grow in entitlement and pride, believing that someone else will always fix things for them. No discipline seems good at the time (flashbacks to long summers slamming doors as an angry teenager, shaking my fist and saying choice words to my parents), but in the end we know that it produces a harvest of righteousness and peace.

> In your struggle against sin, you have not yet resisted to the point of shedding your blood. And have you completely forgotten this word of encouragement that addresses you as a father addresses his son? It says,
>
> > "My son, do not make light of the Lord's discipline,
> > *and do not lose heart when he rebukes you,*

because the Lord disciplines the one he loves,
and he chastens everyone he accepts as his son."

Endure hardship as discipline; God is treating you as his children. For what children are not disciplined by their father? If you are not disciplined—and everyone undergoes discipline—then you are not legitimate, not true sons and daughters at all. Moreover, we have all had human fathers who disciplined us and we respected them for it. *How much more should we submit to the Father of spirits and live!* They disciplined us for a little while as they thought best; but *God disciplines us for our good, in order that we may share in his holiness. No discipline seems pleasant at the time, but painful. Later on, however, it produces a harvest of righteousness and peace for those who have been trained by it.* (Heb. 12:4–11)

So, in summary, don't make light of discipline when it comes your way, and don't lose heart when God rebukes you—get excited! Those cracks in the foundation? Let Him expose them and heal them. You're about to bear some good fruit. Remember that He disciplines those He loves and corrects everyone He accepts as His child. What a gift! So, choose to persevere through hardship, learn from it, grow in it, let it humble you. Remember, if our imperfect earthly fathers disciplined us, how much more should we submit to the discipline of the Father of spirits and find life to the full? Yes, at the time, walking through discipline is the worst, painful even—but it brings about what we've been praying for in our lives: a harvest of righteousness and peace!

In this chapter, we're going to slow ourselves down and learn from the changes we've walked through. Reflect, understand, and move forward. As you sit here and read these words, maybe you've moved cities and your relationships have changed drastically, for better or for worse. You may have lost someone you deeply love or found yourself in the middle of a heartbreaking divorce. You may have outgrown the job you've been in for years, and now know it's time for a change. Or you simply may be choosing change because your mental, emotional, physical, and spiritual health demand it. Wherever you find yourself as you read these words, I pray the path forward will be made clear as you open your heart to learn from God after all you've been through.

May the final verses of Psalm 139 be our prayer:

> Search me, God, and know my heart;
>   test me and know my anxious thoughts.
> See if there is any offensive way in me,
>   and lead me in the way everlasting. (vv. 23–24)

STOP AND REFLECT

B. B. King said, "The beautiful thing about learning is that nobody can take it away from you."[1] Learning equals growth.

When we brave change, the *hope* is that we learn from our success and failure, that we slow down enough to stop, reflect, learn, and in turn, grow.

As I began to write this book, I knew that I only had my own experiences to draw from. I started to talk to close friends and family members to ask how they've braved and walked through all types of change. I also digitally crowdsourced, asking people to share what they had learned and how they grew through some of their greatest mountaintop and valley seasons of life. At the very core of their growth, a deeper intimacy was found with God. This seemed to be the redemptive thread through it all. They were fortified and strengthened and ultimately fell more in love with Jesus.

I discovered that some found growth in relationship with Jesus, depth in true godly community, and, ultimately, healing.

Others discovered a tender closeness with God coupled with a prevailing need to seek His guidance while navigating the uncharted territory laid out before them. Some found out through the insatiable storms, while the wind, waves, and torrents battered their lives, that their house actually *was* built on the Rock. Many found the need to intentionally develop and trust their own discernment more quickly due to relational pain because not everyone is who they say they are, and underdeveloped discernment propagates cycles of pain and betrayal. Others matured through pain and change, finding an increase of faith paired with a desire to genuinely surrender and a sincere joy while doing so. Some found personal transformation not only in their relationship with Jesus but also in their relationship with their spouse and in their friendships. In the midst of the valleys, others found God for the first time and received Jesus, gaining a church family and loving community to walk with. Storms, change, pruning, cutting off, shaking, awakening, valleys, mountaintops, and fiery furnaces all have the potential to refine us. When we choose to humbly learn, our character can incrementally grow, producing the fruit of wisdom.

GARNERING WISDOM

Wisdom is often gained in two ways: from personal experience and from watching another's personal experience and making different choices to carve out a healthier path. Acquiring wisdom is essential as we learn from the changes we walk through with each new season. Personally, I'd rather not take the same test time and time again.

Raising our kids in New York City for twelve years was incredible. We'd moved from Australia in 2010 when we only had three little ones—five, three, and two at the time. A few years later, we had our fourth. New York is a city of opportunity: the museums, the people, the schools, the parks, the culture, Broadway, the ability to walk to everything or jump on a subway to get there. Everything was at our fingertips. That said, kids in New York grow up quickly riding the subway alone to middle school and high school from twelve years of age, seeing, hearing, and being aware of much more than the average adolescent (those posters in the subway advertising the Sex Museum and *so* much more).

Paul and I knew from the time we arrived there that we were going to need to be intentional in how we discipled our children at home to encourage them to gain wisdom from their faith and the Word and not *always* from painful experiences. Yes, experience is a wonderful teacher, but if we can learn from other people's mistakes or from the wisdom that "cries out in the street" (Prov. 1:20 NRSVuc) in my opinion, it's a better option and a lot less painful.

Paul and I heard from a mentor years ago "the rule of first mention," which means let your kids hear it from you first, whether "it" is about sex and sexuality, pornography, how babies are made, marriage, theology, politics— anything you know they'll be taught or gleaning from others in a (public) school environment, through electronics, or through the overheard conversations of others. Do your best to talk to them about it first so that when they learn things that are outside of a biblical worldview, you're already set up to have meaningful conversations without fear, teaching them to think critically and grow healthily one day at a time.

A few of the things Paul and I have done with our children—as well as in our own lives to continue to be students and hopefully acquire greater wisdom as we brave continual change—are having regular family dinners, reading through the book of Proverbs regularly, and reading through the Bible from start to finish.

We fight to carve out space for family dinners in our household. The older and busier my kids get, the harder it is to nail down a time. And I am keenly aware with each passing day that they'll soon be moved out, studying, married, and giving me grandchildren. Each season, the day or time that we gather for family dinner changes, but it's a priority for everyone each week. I hope that when we're old and our kids have kids, we'll still be coming together each week to have dinner and meaningful conversations.

When we sit at the table, no phones are present, not in our pockets or within grabbing distance. We do the same when we go out to eat because phones tend to be a barricade to intimacy. As we come together, we take turns sharing our highs and lows, actively listening to one another, and doing our very best not to interrupt or cross talk. We place value on the one who is sharing and know the same honor will be given to us when our turn comes. Of course, we don't do this perfectly, but it is our goal. We glean so much wisdom and life from one another. This is the place where no topic is off-limits. We learn empathy, honesty, and how to actively listen and hear one another.

We have also gone through a time as a family when, every Saturday morning, we'd read a Proverb out loud together, journal about it with worship music on, and then share what we learned, followed by prayer (usually a short prayer). We talked about (and lived) the value of gleaning wisdom from God as we all continued to navigate living in a broken and fallen world. Since then, I've watched one of my children read the whole of Proverbs over and over again with a holy desperation to gain understanding and resist the foolishness of the world. I love how Proverbs 1:5 says, "Let the wise hear and increase in learning, and the one who understands obtain guidance" (ESV). And Proverbs 18:15 reminds us, "An intelligent heart acquires knowledge, and the ear of the wise seeks knowledge" (ESV). As we brave change, may we be people who continue to cry out for wisdom and understanding. May we acquire knowledge from the Word and lean into the whisper of the Holy Spirit with obedience. Abigail Adams said, "Learning is not attained by chance, it must be sought for with ardour and attended to with diligence."[2]

Last, one of the things we do in our household to acquire wisdom is to encourage our teenagers to read the Bible from start to finish at least once before they move out so they can see the full story of God, His redemptive plan, and how they have been redeemed and adopted in. I am constantly blown away by what they see and understand and how it shapes their lives. Our prayer is that we teach them that the times change, but the Word of God is not only timeless, it's *timely*. They will have struggles, pain, challenges, change, and loss that they'll have to navigate as they mature. We pray that we've given them the tools to walk these out with God and others to grow in wisdom, integrity, and discernment, learning from the storms they've weathered to help them become better sailors on the wild waters of change.

LEARNING TO TAKE OWNERSHIP (MORE QUICKLY)

Not much lights my fuse as quickly as watching someone shift blame and refuse to take ownership of their life. When someone acts powerless to change (and blames you or someone else for it) *and then* refuses to forgive—someone get a fire hose to cool me off *stat*! Let the record show that I know I'm not perfect in this either. But one thing I do know is that we cannot change if we don't take ownership of what we have the ability to take ownership of. Sounds simple, but day after day we have to willingly lay down our pride to see lasting transformation in Christ. We have a God who has come to make us whole—spirit, soul, and body—through the finished work on the cross. But if we refuse to walk *with* Him and work *with* Him in our sanctification, then we remain the same or, even worse, regress.

In 2 Samuel 11, we read the story of David and Bathsheba. It starts off, "*In the spring*, at the time when kings go off to war, David sent Joab out with the king's men and the whole Israelite army. They destroyed the Ammonites and besieged Rabbah. *But David remained in Jerusalem*" (v. 1). In the springtime, kings were meant to be off at war. King David stayed home, and that one choice was a catalyst for disaster. His hands were prepared for battle, yet remaining stationary at home left him open to temptation. If he hadn't sent others out to do the job he was meant to do, then he wouldn't have been on his roof watching Bathsheba, the wife of Uriah (one of his warriors), as she bathed. David's messengers go and get her, he sleeps with her, and she becomes pregnant. Shortly after, David hatches a plan to bring her husband home to sleep with her so that he'll think it's his child. But Uriah, acting as an honorable warrior in the season of war, doesn't go home but sleeps at the entrance to the palace with the servants of his master (David).

When David asks why he doesn't go home to his wife, Uriah says, "The ark and Israel and Judah are staying in tents, and my commander Joab and my lord's men are camped in the open country. How could I go to my house to eat and drink and make love to my wife? As surely as you live, I will not do such a thing!" (2 Sam. 11:11). David tries to get him drunk and again make him go home to his wife, but Uriah does no such thing. As Uriah goes back to the battlefield, David sends word to Joab to put Uriah in a place where the strongest battle will be in hopes that he will die, and that is exactly what happens. So David not only commits adultery but also premeditated murder.

I'm not sure if David thought he'd gotten away with it or not, but God saw, and it grieved His heart. Second Samuel 11:27 says that "the thing David had done displeased the LORD." In chapter 12, the prophet Nathan shows up at David's door and confronts him by telling him a story about a rich man and a poor man in the same town. In essence, the rich man has all he needs, and the poor man has only a little lamb that he has bought and raised and that has grown up with him and his children. It has shared his food, drank from his cup, and even slept in his arms. The ewe has been like a daughter to him. Verse 4 says, "Now a traveler came to the rich man, but the rich man refrained from taking one of his own sheep or cattle to prepare a meal for the traveler who had come to him. Instead, he took the ewe lamb that belonged to the poor man and prepared it for the one who had come to him."

When David hears this story, he is furious, burning with anger and ready to put the man to death who did this. But Nathan says, "You are the man!" (v. 7). He goes on to say some pretty difficult things to David, telling him direct consequences of his foolish actions. David is filled with sorrow and deep grief for his sin and says to the prophet, "I have sinned against the LORD" (v. 13). This moment changes everything for David. At the end of verse 13, Nathan says, "The LORD has taken away your sin. You are not going to die."

Out of this destructive series of choices come adultery, death, rebuke, and repentance, as well as what we now know as Psalm 51. A psalm of confession, repentance, and mercy written by King David.

> Create in me a pure heart, O God,
>   and renew a steadfast spirit within me.
> Do not cast me from your presence
>   or take your Holy Spirit from me.
> Restore to me the joy of your salvation
>   and grant me a willing spirit, to sustain me. (vv. 10–12)

These words are a plea from a sorrowful heart that longs to be restored to purity after sin and foolish choices. David could be called "a man after God's own heart" because he took owner-ship, repented, and changed his ways. May we allow transition, brave change, pain, and even foolish choices to be wise teachers that cause us to quickly own our stuff and be transformed in the process.

TEACHABILITY, HUMILITY, AND BLIND SPOTS

Some of the most practical ways I continue to learn from change and transition are by choosing to remain teachable no matter what, choosing humility (hopefully before I'm humbled by the Lord), and allowing trusted people in my life to lovingly call out my blind spots. I mentioned in chapter 4 that part of my game plan was to be part of a Celebrate Recovery Step Study group with Irene as well as other pastors and church leaders. It was a place where I could do all of the above and then some. I learned something new every time we gathered together. I had to decide to humble myself weekly and tell the truth about where I was really at, allowing others into my life when a part of me wanted to keep them out. And I gave these women the place to call me out too, because we'd created a place of safety to do so.

There's a prayer that we'd often pray together in our Step Study group:

Prayer for Serenity

God, grant me the serenity
to accept the things I cannot change,
the courage to change the things I can,
and the wisdom to know the difference.
Living one day at a time,
enjoying one moment at a time;
accepting hardship as a pathway to peace;

taking, as Jesus did,
this sinful world as it is,
not as I would have it;
trusting that You will make all things right
if I surrender to Your will;
so that I may be reasonably happy in this life
and supremely happy with You forever in the next.
Amen.[3]

Acceptance, courage, wisdom, weathering hardship, surrender ... that we would continue to learn these vital truths, building our life on the Rock as we persevere one day at a time.

LET'S TALK ABOUT GOOD CHANGE

Most change is hard, but let's remember that there is good change too.

Israel's deliverance from Egypt was a good change, but as we've read, they often struggled to see that it was good. They wanted to go back to their "meat pots" instead of being provided manna and quail by the God of the universe. They saw God physically deliver them from their captors by some of the most spectacular signs and wonders recorded in all of history, yet they wondered if God had brought them out in the wilderness to die. Haven't we all been like this? Finding ourselves in the midst of answered prayer but crying out to God for another way?

How often do we miss the good change right in front of us because we're longing for the best parts of what used to be? Meanwhile, God is gently trying to nudge us along with an abundance of patience and loving-kindness that I cannot comprehend.

In the middle of writing this book, my husband and I had a long check-in chat one morning after a heavy season of travel. We needed to reconnect and recalibrate, and I'd pretty much started a fight the night before because I had felt distant from him. He got up early the next morning to reflect on how he was really doing in the midst of the massive life change we were in. There was a long list of discoveries in his excavation, many of which resonated with me. So much good change had taken place that we didn't fully recognize the loss and grief buried right below the surface in both of our hearts. When you're in a season of "new" and it *is* good, the growth points and waves of grief tend to hit unexpectedly. For us, it was the morning after our first small-group Christmas party with new friends.

The night before, we had sat around a table with people who are God's kindness to us. After years of pastoring a church, I don't think we'd ever imagined a friend group like this and hadn't fully realized just how lonely we'd been. Yes, we had a handful of close, beautiful, lifelong friends from our years pastoring in the city, but this small group of humans welcoming us into their ten-plus years of friendship surprisingly brought us both to a breaking point. Not because it was bad but because it was so good. Too good. We realized what we'd really lost in leaving what we'd had in New York: the life we'd built, the friends we'd made, the life our kids had had, the church, and the changed lives. And we also realized what we'd never had.

When Paul started to share that morning, I found myself in a pool of tears. The kind of crying where it's hard to catch your breath and the throbbing in your chest feels like it might just crack your sternum wide open. I was wadding up tissues so quickly that my own miniature Mount Everest was forming on the ground as I tossed them aside. We realized that we both felt the ache of good change. We had so much gratitude, and we felt the tension of heartache for the loss of the good things as well as for the confusing and difficult things we'd left behind.

It was all in contrast to something so divine right in front of us: a group of people embracing us into the fold.

The whole night after the Christmas party, I slept restlessly. Every time I was conscious, I would hear this voice in my head: *You don't deserve this . . . You don't belong here . . .* Fully aware of where that voice was coming from, I rejected the lie, but I still had to understand that, like the Israelites, I wasn't sure if I would fully fit or belong. I was at an impasse: Do I receive the goodness of God even though I need to grieve and walk through the necessary steps to get to a place of acceptance? Or do I reject it all before it rejects me? Do I mistake the pain of change and loss for punishment? Or understand that it simply comes with the territory of being human? And can I see the good right in front of me, even as I leave behind what used to be?

Good change and transformation will continually come into our lives as we choose to abide in Christ no matter what we face. Many a season, I've heard the Lord whisper to my heart when I'm longing for another word: *Remain.*

Sometimes that's our only directive.

It is the only way to bear fruit.

I am the true vine, and my Father is the gardener. He cuts off every branch in me that bears no fruit, while every branch that does bear fruit he prunes so that it will be even more fruitful. You are already clean because of the word I have spoken to you. *Remain* in me, as I also remain in you. No branch can bear fruit by itself; it must *remain* in the vine. Neither can you bear fruit unless you *remain* in me.

I am the vine; you are the branches. If you *remain* in me and I in you, you will bear much fruit; apart from me you can do nothing. If you do not *remain* in me, you are like a branch that is thrown away and withers; such branches are picked up, thrown into the fire and burned. If you *remain* in me and my words *remain* in you, ask whatever you wish, and it will be done for you. This is to my Father's glory, that you bear much fruit, showing yourselves to be my disciples. (John 15:1–8)

When you're waiting on God for direction, remain.

When you don't know what to do, remain.

When you walk through excruciating pain, remain.

When others receive what you've prayed for, remain.

When you wonder if the storm will ever end, remain.

When walking through a loss feels insurmountable, remain.

When you get all that you've ever dreamed of, remain.

When you still have unanswered questions, remain.

When you're welcomed into loving, godly community, remain.

When you walk through the darkest valley, remain.

Remain.

We learn the deep and simple things as we remain.

Good change, hard change, God change comes as we *choose* to remain—no matter what.

BUILDING ON THE ROCK

Scripture Meditation: Psalm 139:23–24

> Search me, God, and know my heart;
> test me and know my anxious thoughts.
> See if there is any offensive way in me,
> and lead me in the way everlasting.

Take a moment and be still before God. Speak this psalm out loud as a prayer. What does the Holy Spirit whisper to you? What is coming to mind? What things are being revealed in your heart?

REFLECTION QUESTIONS

- How did you grow through your most recent change? What did you learn? Take some time to reflect on the goodness of God. Celebrate the wins, even among the losses.
- What good change are you in the middle of and how do you personally safeguard against rejecting what God is giving to you?

GUIDED PRAYER

Today, our guided prayer will be the "Prayer for Serenity." Take it in. Pray it with a group if you're doing this book together. Write or print it out and put it up somewhere.

Prayer for Serenity

God, grant me the serenity
to accept the things I cannot change,
the courage to change the things I can,
and the wisdom to know the difference.
Living one day at a time,
enjoying one moment at a time;
accepting hardship as a pathway to peace;
taking, as Jesus did,

this sinful world as it is,
not as I would have it;
trusting that You will make all things right
if I surrender to Your will;
so that I may be reasonably happy in this life
and supremely happy with You forever in the next.
Amen.[4]

CHAPTER 6

CHOOSE TO KEEP SHOWING UP

To learn strong faith is to endure great trials. I have learned
my faith by standing firm amid severe testings.

George Müller

Experiencing transition in life can be like riding a roller coaster:
either you don't get on, or you choose to and ride it out until the
end.

I know I've caught myself reading the parting of the Red Sea
like it's a bedtime story. Yet when I really go there, I cannot fathom
the perseverance and resilience it took to keep walking forward
when all I'd want to do is curl up in a ball, crippled with fear, or
run back into captivity.

Imagine with me for a moment actually being in that crowd
of weary people. You've just escaped Egypt with all that you own
and are able to carry. You've witnessed back-to-back plagues ravage the Egyptian people while you were protected and set apart.
Then you're told to ask the Egyptians for articles of silver, gold,

and clothing because "the LORD had made the Egyptians favorably disposed toward the people, and they gave them what they asked for" (Exod. 12:36). As you leave Rameses and travel to Sukkoth, you look around to see "six hundred thousand men on foot, besides women and children" (v. 37). Livestock are bumping into you, and everyone is carrying dough without yeast in it because there was no time to prepare food for the journey.

I imagine that if I were in their shoes, I'd be replaying all that just transpired as I took each step toward a new life. The shocking death of all of the Egyptian firstborn children, the protection of the Israelites' own firstborn children, the inaugural Passover feast, and the following consecration of their families' firstborn livestock. And then they walk in obedience, step-by-step on a dry, dusty desert path in the midst of a massive deliverance from generations-long captivity, trusting that Moses's word was from God. They come to a halt when they stumble upon the Red Sea. The absolute terror and anger that must've risen to the surface, especially when they realized that they were being chased by Pharaoh's horses and chariots, horsemen and troops.

> As Pharaoh approached, the Israelites looked up, and there were the Egyptians, marching after them. They were terrified and cried out to the LORD. They said to Moses, "Was it because there were no graves in Egypt that you brought us to the desert to die? What have you done to us by bringing us out of Egypt? Didn't we say to you in Egypt, 'Leave us alone; let us serve the Egyptians'? It would have been better for us to serve the Egyptians than to die in the desert!"
>
> Moses answered the people, "Do not be afraid. Stand firm and you will see the deliverance the LORD will bring you today. The Egyptians you see today you will never see again. The LORD will fight for you; you need only to be still." (14:10–14)

This sounds like a ridiculous game plan. I can only imagine the outrage: "Be still? Stand firm? Trust God? He'll fight for us? We have nowhere to run!" Then Moses raises his staff and stretches out his hand over the Red Sea and everyone holds their breath. "Then the angel of God, who had been traveling in front of Israel's army, withdrew and went behind them. The pillar of cloud also moved from in front and stood behind them, coming between the armies of Egypt and Israel" (vv. 19–20). And then it happened. A strong east wind started to steadily blow, turning the Red Sea into dry land before the very eyes of the Israelites. "The waters were divided, and the Israelites went through the sea on dry ground, with a wall of water on their right and on their left" (vv. 21–22). After the whole of Israel had passed through on dry ground, one motion of Moses's outstretched hand over the sea, and the Lord enclosed it on top of the pursuing Egyptian army. "And when the Israelites saw the mighty hand of the LORD displayed against the Egyptians, the people feared the LORD and put their trust in him and in Moses his servant" (v. 31). See, not a sweet little bedtime story but a holy and terrifying exodus into a new season.

How do we as a people stand firm and let the Lord fight for us as we step into what is new? How do we do this in a life-altering season that causes us to ask questions that may remain unanswered? How do we trust that God will part the waters of our figurative Red Sea so that we can walk across on dry ground?

While navigating multiple changes and transitions all at once, I happened to be in the midst of reading *Secrets of the Secret Place* by Bob Sorge. These two paragraphs were a revelatory word in this particular season for me, and I hope they will be for you too:

> The only way through is to make a decision in advance that no matter how tough the slogging gets, we're never going to give up on our pursuit of God. We're going to abide in Christ no matter what.

I'll let you in on a secret: This kind of tenacious commitment to endurance will open the path to the most meaningful dimensions of relationship with the Lord.

Seasons not only break the monotony of sameness, they are necessary to productivity. Nothing can live in unbroken sunshine. Constant joy and happiness, with no clouds on the horizon, produces drought. Night is as important as day; the sun must be followed by clouds and rain. Nonstop sunshine only creates a desert. We don't enjoy storms, but they're an essential part of a complete life, and the key to victory comes in the finding how to weather the storms of life in such a way that they don't dislodge us from our secret life in God.[1]

We need to decide in advance that we will commit to pursuing God no matter how difficult things get. Building on the Rock, on Jesus, is the only way to keep showing up, to persevere, and to make it through. I've talked to so many people—friends, loved ones, and family—who have made the choice not to be moved no matter what, whether they're navigating one of the biggest challenges they've ever faced or a shocking shift, an unexpected transition, or a dark night of the soul. I had one friend who, in the middle of some of her greatest pain, said, "Where else would I go? What else would I do? Jesus is my everything." Does that mean that the road was peaceful and easy? No. Quite the opposite. Her pursuit of Jesus was what kept her from shattering into a thousand tiny pieces in her darkest hour. Her unwavering love of God was constant even when nothing or no one else was.

The second half of this book will point to our ability to make powerful choices that cause us to welcome growth and trust where God is leading us. These are choices that no one else can make for us but that we must continually choose to make for ourselves. The decision to keep showing up doesn't just happen.

When your Red Sea stands in front of you, or when leaving all you've ever known is the right choice, or when you're left picking up the pieces, wondering what just happened, the choice to persevere will transform you and set you apart. We finish our race on this earth not by coming in first but by staying in our lane and enduring until the end.

CHOOSE NOT TO NEGLECT THIS ONE THING

As a pastor, one of the most heartbreaking parts of leading through 2020 was the lockdown. Losing the gathering of the saints was no small thing, and it did a number on so many of us. People walked away from God, questioned everything, or began a deconstruction journey without reconstructing on Jesus. Marriages fell apart, people who never thought they would had affairs, jobs were lost, hopes were dashed, and people were forced to carve out a new trajectory. Friends became foes, churches were split or closed down, and our relationships were never the same. As we sat at home staring at screens a little too long, the novelty of lockdown wearing off, addictions became a cultural norm—even joked about on social media. Depression and mental health issues rose at heartbreaking levels. Gossip, slander, and the general tearing down of one another from behind a screen without biblical Matthew 18 confrontation, reconciliation, and restoration battered and bruised the bride of Christ.

I understand that 2020 hit us all differently, and it's a year we'd all like to forget, but it did touch us all. One thing is for sure: it changed the landscape of the church. It made me forever thankful for the gathering of believers. Sundays, Wednesdays, discipleship groups, serving together, outreach, you name it—the body of Christ and her mandate on earth to be the hands and feet of Jesus to a lost and broken world were only solidified in my heart as we were each shaken by all that took place. My desire only grew to come together and enthrone God on our praises (Ps. 22:3), encourage one another daily (Heb. 3:13), and be encouraged to go and be the saints who do the work of the ministry (Eph. 4:11–13). The revelation that we are "a holy priesthood, offering spiritual sacrifices acceptable to God through Jesus Christ" (1 Pet. 2:5) was deepened. My understanding of Hebrews was fortified as I studied it together with a group of women. I had always heard people throw around, "Don't give up meeting together, as some are in the habit of doing," when church numbers were down, or people were obviously missing. But reading it in the context of the whole book of Hebrews, written to the newly converted Jewish Christians faltering in their faith partly due to Jewish influences around them (things like still going to a priest to make sacrifices at the temple), helps us to understand how those words affect us now in our day and age.

> Therefore, brothers and sisters, since we have confidence to enter the Most Holy Place by the blood of Jesus, by a new and living way opened for us through the curtain, that is, his body, and since we have a great priest over the house of God, let us draw near to God with a sincere heart and with the full assurance that faith brings, having our hearts sprinkled to cleanse us from a guilty conscience and having our bodies washed with pure water. Let us hold unswervingly to the hope we profess, for he who promised is faithful. And let us consider how we may spur one another on toward love and good deeds, *not giving up meeting together, as some are in the habit of doing*, but encouraging one another—and all the more as you see the Day approaching. (Heb. 10:19–25)

To the Hebrew people, the newfound Christians who had been practicing Jews before the Messiah came, this book was a concise and beautifully written encouragement not to regress or go back to their old ways. To lean in without fear in the face of persecution, remembering that Jesus is superior to the angels, Moses, Joshua, the Hebrew high priest, and all the patriarchs. His sacrifice and resurrection was and is superior. The beginning of Hebrews 10 reminded them that Christ's sacrifice was *once and for all*. There was no need to sacrifice at the temple any longer because the forgiveness of sins was fully given to those who followed in the Way.

"Therefore," verse 19 says, or *because* we are fully forgiven and set free by the finished work on the cross, we should live in such a way that we know we can confidently enter the Most Holy Place because of the blood of Jesus Christ. That no matter what we've done, we can draw near to God "having our hearts sprinkled to cleanse us from a guilty conscience and having our bodies washed with pure water" (v. 22). We are then encouraged not to let go of hope no matter what happens because Jesus is always faithful. Oh, and to "spur one another on toward love and good deeds" (v. 24). And we know that the only way this happens is in relationship. So therefore, as verse 25 tells us, don't give up meeting together "as some are in the habit of doing" (see, context matters). And the "but" that comes after that reminds us to encourage one another all the more as we see "the Day" approaching. The Day of Christ's return for the bride. The bride that we're all a part of.

Gathering together matters. And when we're walking through hell in the midst of our darkest hour, the saints are there to hold us up, to come alongside and love us as we choose to open up and continue to build our lives upon the Rock. God can redeem things in ways we never could've imagined.

THE CHOICE TO PERSEVERE AND THE PRODUCT IT PRODUCES

You know what's underrated? Consistency. My parents are my heroes. Year after year, they're consistent. Faithful. I know I can call them for prayer and they'll actually pray. They wake early every morning to read the Word and get into the presence of God. I have distinct childhood memories of walking up our 1980s brown-shag-carpeted stairs from my room in the basement, fire roaring, coffee brewing, bacon popping, and my parents praying. They'd be sitting in chairs by the fire with their Bibles open, leaning into the presence of God. It's a simple imprint in my mind that changed my life.

As an adult, now knowing more of my parents' heartbreaking story and what they both walked through during my childhood, adolescent, and teenage years, I am astounded by their faithfulness to God and one another. It's a miracle. They're a miracle. Their pursuit of God and one another was and is a daily choice. They were in their own desert for twenty-plus years yet still woke early every morning to seek God, hoping that one day they'd be able to set foot on their personal promised land. I can say with confidence that they have now seen the goodness of God in the land of the living, even when it looked like it might not happen. They've never wavered in their faith—they have trusted God even though pain was their portion for years on end.

They've carved out a well-worn path, but only after years of continually doing the one thing that works: pursuing Christ daily. The trials and testing of our faith are inevitable. So how do we respond to those things with the consistency, faithfulness, and perseverance that bring about a maturity and oneness with Christ that cannot be explained unless one has tasted and seen it for themselves? When we figure this out, pure joy is found.

Consider it *pure joy*, my brothers and sisters, whenever you face *trials* of many kinds, because you know that the *testing of your faith* produces *perseverance*. Let perseverance finish its work so that you may be *mature and complete, not lacking anything*. If any of you lacks wisdom, you should ask God, who gives generously to all without finding fault, and it will be given to you. But when you ask, you must believe and not doubt, because the one who doubts is like a wave of the sea, blown and tossed by the wind. That person should not expect to receive anything from the Lord. Such a person is double-minded and unstable in all they do. (James 1:2–8)

We spend most of our lives avoiding tests and hard things. When we drive somewhere, we want the quickest route, obviously. When we want to get healthy, we'd like a pill to do the trick for us, but we know it's going to require incremental changes and then consistent, daily choices to do all the things that bring about health in our lives. When a hard conversation needs to be had or a tough situation presents itself at work, sometimes we'd like the problem to solve itself or disappear—unless you're a born confronter, then you love this stuff. We avoid tests if we can, but I've learned that if we don't sit the faith test that we find ourselves bumping up against in the season we're in, we'll probably face it again in the next one.

I hated taking tests in school, and that has definitely carried on into adulthood. I got my license when I turned sixteen but, in the process, failed the written test (the most commonsense test ever) and had to come back and do it again, passing it by the skin of my teeth. I was so embarrassed. In my early twenties I moved to Sydney, Australia, and had to forfeit my US license to get an Australian one. After living there for ten years and then moving back stateside to New York City, my US license had expired, which meant I needed to take the written test again *and* take a driving test. I'd already been down that embarrassing road, so I made a conscious decision to avoid it. I explained away (mainly to myself) for eleven years why I didn't need to get my license in NYC. I mean, I walked, rode the subway, took a taxi, or called an Uber, so therefore no need. And if we needed to rent a car as a family, my husband could drive. I landlocked myself and stole my own freedom by avoiding a test for eleven years, and in the process, I put all the driving pressure for our family on my husband. And then God changed our assignment. We transitioned the church, stepped out of our roles, and prepared to move to Charleston, South Carolina, where I would have to have my license to simply live. You can't get eggs or a gallon of milk without driving somewhere. So, I bit the bullet and ended up taking a driving course in New York. I took driving lessons in one of those humiliating driving-school cars with a big, triangular sign on top. To my surprise, I passed the test with flying colors. What in the world had I been waiting for? What had I been avoiding? Failure, shame, embarrassment . . . that's what.

Tests are the worst, and having our faith tested can be difficult and painful. But we see in James 1 that when we face a trial that tests our faith, our choice to persevere produces something beautiful. When perseverance finishes its work, we become "mature and complete, not lacking anything" (v. 4). This is where we find *pure*, unadulterated joy. We don't expect others to give us what only Jesus can. When change, trials, testing, pain, seasons we never saw coming, or life transitions take us by surprise, Jesus is our constant. Don't avoid the tests.

Remember that His faithfulness and love complete us. In Him we lack no good thing.

KEEP RUNNING YOUR RACE

So, keep running your race. Keep a guard over your heart, not allowing yourself to envy another's lane, because when you do, you'll veer off course. I said it earlier and I'll say it here again to remind our souls, we finish our race on this earth not by coming in first but by staying in our lane and enduring until the end.

My husband hates running with a passion. In this context, *hate* is not too strong of a word. When he and a group of six men were about to embark on a hunt camp in the Montana wilderness without the help of professional guides, they all knew they needed increased physical training that would take them to a new level of endurance. They didn't need strength training as much as they needed endurance training. So one of the men put a challenge out there for the group to run one hundred miles before they went on the trip.

I watched my husband get out and run every single day—rain, heavy, blanket-like Charleston humidity, or shine—literally. Over and over again, it would start pouring rain during the window of time he had to get his miles in. Nevertheless, he'd suit up, put on his headphones, and go out. It started to become a time of prayer for him as well. Not only was he enduring physically, but he was also choosing to endure spiritually and pray over others. He hit his goal and we all celebrated and felt challenged too. It was really cool for the kids and me to watch. The choice to endure and face the challenge in front of him, even though most days he didn't *feel* like it, not only got him physically ready for the hunt camp in the Montana wilderness but also changed him from the inside out.

Dietrich Bonhoeffer writes, "To endure the cross is not tragedy; it is the suffering which is the fruit of an exclusive allegiance to Jesus Christ."[2] We have an aversion to endurance and perseverance in our faith journey because the flesh gets loud and wants what it wants. Fasting, prayer, the Word, spiritual disciplines, and taking care of our body, the temple of the Holy Spirit, remind us daily that we have been crucified with Christ and that we no longer live but that it is Christ who lives in us.

> Do you not know that in a race all the runners run, but only one gets the prize? *Run in such a way as to get the prize.* Everyone who

competes in the games goes into *strict training*. They do it to get a crown that will not last, but we do it to get a crown that will last forever. Therefore *I do not run like someone running aimlessly*; I do not fight like a boxer beating the air. No, I strike a blow to my body and make it my slave so that after I have preached to others, *I myself will not be disqualified for the prize*. (1 Cor. 9:24–27)

There is no one to please in this race but God, so whom and what are you running for? One way not to be disqualified (in any race) is to keep going and stay in our lane. There are several ways to be disqualified too, like running around the hurdle or obstacle rather than going over it, starting the race before the gun goes off, or stepping in someone else's lane. This is why we must go into "strict training," to receive an eternal crown, not an earthly one. Therefore, to run with focus and perseverance is worth it. Endure until the end. Focus—don't live aimlessly. Don't envy another's "lane." Fix your eyes on Jesus. Keep showing up.

And let us run with perseverance *the race marked out for us*, fixing our eyes on Jesus, the pioneer and perfecter of faith. (Heb. 12:1–2)

There is a race marked out for you and you alone. Fix your eyes. He's got you.

CHOOSE TO BUILD RIGHT *SO THAT* YOU MAY ENDURE

When we were in Israel for my fortieth-birthday trip, walking through Capernaum, I remember our guide saying, "If Jesus was a carpenter, what do you think He built? What materials do you think He used? Look around, what do you see?" We were surrounded by stone structures everywhere we looked, and the thought had honestly never crossed my mind. In the days that

Jesus roamed the earth, the principal material for a carpenter to build a house with would've been stone. And the cornerstone was critical in the building of any structure. Without it, the integrity of the entire building was at risk.

Historically, the cornerstone was the most important part of any building. The total weight of an edifice rested on this particular stone, which, if removed, would collapse the whole structure. The cornerstone was also the key to keeping the walls straight. The builders would take sightings along the edges of this part of the building. If the cornerstone was set properly, the stonemasons could be assured that all the other corners of the building would be at the appropriate angles as well. Thus, the cornerstone became a symbol for that which held life together.[3]

First Peter 2:4–8 says,

As you come *to him, the living Stone*—rejected by humans but chosen by God and precious to him—*you also, like living stones*, are being built into a spiritual house to be a holy priesthood, offering spiritual sacrifices acceptable to God through Jesus Christ. For in Scripture it says:

> "See, I lay a stone in Zion,
> a chosen and precious cornerstone,
> and the one who trusts in him
> will never be put to shame."

The revelation within this passage alone could take us through the fire and back again. When we choose to build our lives on our precious cornerstone, Christ, who gave everything for us, we become like living stones that form a spiritual house, a "holy priesthood," and we offer our lives as spiritual sacrifices to God only through the life, death, and resurrection of Jesus Christ. The daily decision to trust in Him causes us to live without shame.

I mentioned earlier that the Sermon on the Mount covers everything from adultery and murder to judgment and prayer and every heart issue in between. Jesus tells us *and* shows us with His life what a *true* disciple looks like. And, as a reminder, we'll circle back to the scriptural anchor of this book. As Jesus brings this timeless sermon to a close, He says:

> *Therefore everyone who hears these words of mine and puts them into practice is like a wise man who built his house on the rock.* The rain came down, the streams rose, and the winds blew and beat against that house; yet it did not fall, because it had its foundation on the rock. *But everyone who hears these words of mine and does not put them into practice is like a foolish man who built his house on sand.* The rain came down, the streams rose, and the winds blew and beat against that house, and it fell with a great crash. (Matt. 7:24–27)

We cannot get away from the reality that what we resolve to build our lives on, come hell or high water, determines how we will weather the storms and walk through difficult or even prayed-for changes in life. To endure, persevere, walk in resilience, and keep showing up as a valued part of the body of Christ is a powerful choice.

BUILDING ON THE ROCK

Scripture Meditation: James 1:2–8

> Consider it pure joy, my brothers and sisters, whenever you face trials of many kinds, because you know that the testing of your

faith produces perseverance. Let perseverance finish its work so that you may be mature and complete, not lacking anything. If any of you lacks wisdom, you should ask God, who gives generously to all without finding fault, and it will be given to you. But when you ask, you must believe and not doubt, because the one who doubts is like a wave of the sea, blown and tossed by the wind. That person should not expect to receive anything from the Lord. Such a person is double-minded and unstable in all they do.

Take a moment and be still before God. Read the passage out loud. What stands out to you? Underline it, reflect on it, journal about it, write it out, and/or pray it through. Let the Scripture read you, change you, and direct you to Jesus.

REFLECTION QUESTIONS

- What tests and trials have you faced or are you facing now that are bringing you to a place of perseverance and, in turn, maturity and completeness? Take a moment to reflect and thank God for how He continues to bring you through.
- Do you struggle with running your own race? Do you tend to envy others or look to them for direction or inspiration rather than the One who created you and shows you how to endure in the lane He's marked out for you? If so, take some time to repent and ask God for fresh clarity and direction.
- How and where can you "keep showing up" even if you don't *feel* like it?

GUIDED PRAYER

Father, thank You for Your grace in and through every season. Thank You for never leaving nor forsaking me when I've been so weary, angry, confused, frustrated, and disappointed. You have truly been a constant stream of goodness and mercy in my life. I am overwhelmed with gratitude at the sheer knowledge that You've never given up on me. From this day forward, I am determined that no matter how difficult life gets, I will not neglect the pursuit of Your heart. Please continue to show me how to build my life on You, and forgive me for the times I've chosen to build my life on shifting sands. Forgive me for the idols I've bowed down to rather than giving You all the glory and honor You deserve. I know You're always with me, and like the Israelites, when there is nothing left to do, I will choose to be still, stand firm, and trust in You, knowing that You will fight for me. The battle is Yours.

CHAPTER 7

CHOOSE INTEGRITY IN CHANGE

> The integrity of the upright guides them,
> but the unfaithful are destroyed by their duplicity.
>
> Proverbs 11:3

Endings happen; they're simply part of the human experience. So how can we choose to process life's major (or minor) transitions with integrity? Integrity is defined as "the quality of being honest and having strong moral principles; moral uprightness."[1] How can we move through change honestly, without getting stuck in a lie, false belief system, or cycle of grief that becomes a detrimental script that we then live by?

On a beautiful, brisk, cloudless January morning in Charleston, I got on a phone call with a friend to touch base and check in with each other. Living in different states, we do this from time to time to make sure we stay connected. She knew I was in the middle of writing this book and asked how far I'd gotten, and it happened to be this very chapter. She, being a certified emotional intelligence coach, got very excited and asked if she could process some ideas. I quickly opened my laptop and took notes because she guides people through change and endings on a regular basis, *and* she's passionate about helping people process with integrity. Not only did I get a free coaching session with a friend, but I'm going to share it with you (with her permission), starting with some thoughts and questions to ponder as you walk through or face a new ending or transition in your life.

PROCESSING CHANGE WITH INTEGRITY

In this section, I'm going to break down each guiding principle in bullet-point form so that you can pause and process each one.

- We all feel pain in change, and how it lands on us depends on varying factors, like family of origin and how they processed pain, past pain (healed or unhealed), lies we've believed (remember, wounds, lies, false beliefs, strongholds, vows, false self), or a lens through which we view pain.
- Pay attention to the pain. When it comes up, it means it's time to deal with something. Feel it. Process it. It won't kill you to touch the pain, and it doesn't go away until it has been processed. Can you label the emotions you feel?
- Ask what is beneath the hurt. We've established the need to grieve, but then we have to *choose* to process the pain with integrity, or we'll find ourselves stuck in a cycle of grief, believing a lie about ourselves or others, unable to move forward. So when you ask yourself what's beneath the hurt, is it the belief of a lie? Or has this particular situation or season triggered the past?

- Believing a lie and playing a script that narrates an untrue story over and over again actually lacks integrity. This is where we find ourselves bearing false witness against a brother or sister in Christ. When you believe a lie about one situation or another, you begin to bear false witness in your heart and often to others (aka gossip). Simply put, this is sin, and it requires our repentance. Scripture tells us, "You shall not bear false witness against your neighbor" (Exod. 20:16 ESV), and "The LORD detests lying lips, but he delights in people who are trustworthy" (Prov. 12:22).

- Remember, even when we *feel* betrayed, we never truly know the motive or intention of another. Only God and the other person know the intentions of their heart.

- We have to be watchful not to vilify someone else for the pain we refuse to process with integrity before God. When we walk through endings, transitions, and major or minor life changes, it's imperative to take ownership of what we can take ownership of. Let God be the righteous judge and jury. Let Him have His justice. Do not try to control the outcome. It never works, and it leaves you exhausted and disappointed.

- Endings, changes, and transitions are opportunities to learn and grow. If we don't, we can get stuck in unhealthy cycles that will repeat themselves. But God can turn things around for good *if* we'll let Him (and stop trying to control the narrative on our end) and *if* we'll process with integrity.

- Ownership changes everything. It also determines the trajectory of our lives. How we choose to respond to perceived rejection and betrayal or even to stark realities—being fired, ignored, or lied about, walking through a relationship falling apart, a huge disturbance in our personal or public lives, and so on—will affect our future. Choosing to navigate life with a pure heart and our integrity intact will save us years of hurt and the need to clean up any messes we have made along the way.

- Finally, remember that our darkest seasons of grief are where much treasure can be found. Isaiah 45:3 says, "And I will give you treasures hidden in the darkness—secret riches. I will do this so you may know that I am the LORD, the God of Israel, the one who calls you by name" (NLT).

The dark times can become Romans 8:28 moments for us, with God using it all for good, if we are willing to go deep and refuse anything less than receiving eternal treasures through the processing of grief. "Treasures," in this context, being anything that God wants to show us or teach us in dark seasons.

HEALTHY AND UNHEALTHY CLOSURE

Being in ministry since 1998, serving at various churches as a volunteer, and being on the staff of and then pastoring a church alongside my husband in New York for over a decade, I've seen a lot of people come and go. I've watched some leave, move, or transition from a church community with deep character and honor in obedience to God, and others who have lacked integrity, damaging and dividing relationships on the way out in an effort to control the narrative. There is a right way and wrong way to walk through any kind of transition, and it's up to us to decide just how we'll do it.

I've heard many people say that the way you leave one season is the way you enter the next one. That quote obviously isn't Scripture, but biblically, we do reap what we sow.

> Do not be deceived: God cannot be mocked. A man reaps what he sows. Whoever sows to please their flesh, from the flesh will reap destruction; whoever sows to please the Spirit, from the Spirit will reap eternal life. Let us not become weary in doing good, for at the proper time we will reap a harvest if we do not give up. Therefore, as we have opportunity, let us do good to all people, especially to those who belong to the family of believers. (Gal. 6:7–10)

We cannot control what others choose to do, but we do get to decide how we journey through the changes we face with integrity (or not). Will we sow to please our flesh or sow to please the Spirit? Because one reaps destruction and the other eternal life. Will we grow weary in doing good and try to take matters into our own hands? Because God's "proper time" for harvest is another outcome we cannot control. As difficult as it may feel at the time, we do still have the ability to choose to pick up our weary feet and keep doing good even when we don't feel like it. And as we leave, transition, face a necessary ending, or navigate change, will we take every opportunity we have to "do good to all people" on our way out, whether it's the difficult close to a season, the end of a marriage, changing roles in a staff position, moving cities, or releasing a child into their next season of life?

The transition you're walking through right now could be connected to a friend or a spouse who has chosen to walk out on you. Maybe you're in an abusive marriage, and you're choosing to make changes for the safety of yourself and your children. Your transition may have to do with a job change, whether you're moving departments, resigning with integrity from a toxic work environment, or simply taking another job as the next step in your career. Maybe you were fired, and the script that's running through your mind due to a lie that's taken root is taking you way off course. Maybe you're moving cities, states, or countries. It's possible you need to cut ties with unhealthy habits, and it's requiring daily changes that are difficult but necessary to bring about the change you want to see in your life. It's encouraging to know that we can make daily biblical choices to do this well and keep our integrity intact.

I SURRENDER ALL

It's good to remember this: We are stewards of everything we have. "The earth is the LORD's, and everything in it" (Ps. 24:1). Our gifts, talents, abilities, marriages, friendships, children, relationships, homes, jobs, finances, and any earthly treasures are stewardship responsibilities—we're literally entitled to zilch. Therefore, a posture of humility and surrender is so important to come against any pride, self-preservation, or entitlement that rises within us in major or minor transitions we walk through so that we can live with open hands and an open and pure heart, yielded to the One who has given us absolutely everything we have.

The opening lyrics to the hymn "I Surrender All" simply say,

> All to Jesus I surrender
> All to Him I freely give
> I will ever love and trust Him
> In His presence daily live.[2]

This posture will keep us throughout every season of life. As I wake, I surrender all to Jesus. As I wrestle, all to Him I freely give (even though I want to control things). Even when I don't understand how or why I find myself here (wherever "here" is), I will love and trust Him with my life because He knows the beginning from the end. And above all else, I will not forsake the pursuit of Christ; I will acknowledge and live in His presence daily.

Matthew 16:24–27 says,

> Then Jesus said to his disciples, *"Whoever wants to be my disciple must deny themselves and take up their cross and follow me. For whoever wants to save their life will lose it, but whoever loses their life for me will find it. What good will it be for someone to gain the whole world, yet forfeit their soul?* Or what can anyone give in exchange for their soul? For the Son of Man is going to come in his Father's glory with his angels, and then he will reward each person according to what they have done."

The flesh wants what the flesh wants. This is why a lifestyle of denying *our* way is required to live with integrity in our pursuit of Christ and *His* way. In our pursuit of the Spirit, our flesh loves to try to resurrect itself after we've crucified it. Just try fasting for a few days and you'll quickly be reminded how loud it gets. We have to ask ourselves, Am I willing to lose my life and all that I want to grip onto, and all that I perceive I'm entitled to, to find my life in Christ and Christ alone? Can I confidently say what the apostle Paul says in Philippians 3:7–8, "But whatever gain I had, I counted as loss for the sake of Christ. Indeed, *I count everything as loss because of the surpassing worth of knowing Christ Jesus my Lord.* For his sake I have suffered the loss of all things and count them as rubbish, in order that I may gain Christ" (ESV)? How badly do we want to surrender all for the prize that is found in Christ and Christ alone?

Surrendering to Christ keeps us honest. When we're truly yielded to the Holy Spirit, we'll embody a lifestyle of repentance and integrity. Another definition for integrity is "the state of being whole and undivided."[3] When was the last time you braved a storm "undivided," with an abandoned trust in Jesus that, no matter what, He had your back, even when the earthly outcomes weren't all that you'd hoped for?

CHOOSE TO KEEP DOING GOOD, EVEN WHEN OTHERS DON'T

It can become tiresome doing the right thing when others choose not to. And we can be downright vicious to one another in the body of Christ. But Galatians 6:9–10 says,

> *Let us not become weary in doing good,* for at the proper time we will reap a harvest if we do not give up. Therefore, as we have opportunity, *let us do good to all people,* especially to those who belong to the family of believers.

Yes, please, by all means, love the lost, go after the one, but also do good to those who belong to the family of believers because we are *one* body. Remember, if we sow from the flesh, we reap destruction, and if we sow from the Spirit, we reap eternal life. In some respects, the church is center stage in a world that wants to tear it right down. All eyes are on our response to different world events, how we treat the lost, broken, and ostracized, and how we treat one another. The Word tells us that no matter what shaking, or assault, comes at the church, the gates of hell will not prevail (Matt. 16:18) against her because Christ is the chief cornerstone to an eternal structure that will remain after all is said and done. Therefore, as a broken world watches on and the discouraged Christian fights for their faith to remain pure, remember these words from Jesus: "A new command I give you: Love one another. As I have loved you, so you must love one another. By this everyone will know that you are my disciples, if you love one another" (John 13:34–35).

We can say, post, spout, or hashtag #LoveOneAnother, which usually means, "Love me how I want to be loved" or "Love how I love because, in my humble opinion, it's superior to how you love" (been there, done that), but Jesus says for us to love one another *"as I have loved you."*

Do we remember what it was like when we were a wreck and Jesus loved us even though there was no merit for us to be loved in such a pure and profound way? Can we recall what it was like when Jesus rescued us and made us whole even though we didn't deserve for Him to lay down His life for us while we were still sinners? Do we truly remember that wild, radical, unstoppable love? And then, once we do remember it and are consumed with awe because of His grace and mercy, can we take steps to "love one another" as Christ commanded? Can we love others as we have been loved by Him?

It's like Jesus is holding us by the shoulders and lovingly looking us in the eyes, saying, "Oh, I know they don't deserve it (and neither do you), but love them anyway because that's how I love you."

(Plays unhealthy script in mind.) "But God, I want them to love *me*, love *my* way, love how *I* see things, agree with *me*; that's what love means to *me*."

No, that's not what love is or means . . . *"As I have loved you. . . .* By this everyone will know you are my disciples." There is a different standard for Christ followers. We get to lay down our lives for one another despite what others do or how they think, feel, or even act. And you may not receive love back, but you get to choose your move. You can love with boundaries. Love them even when they "know not what they do" (Luke 23:34 ESV) or when they 100 percent know exactly what they're doing. This is a laid-down love. This is a love that causes the world to take notice of the true disciples of Christ.

"TO YOU WHO ARE LISTENING"

Walking through transition requires levels of forgiveness that can feel like a battle of the will to tap into but will help us as we choose integrity in life's major and minor changes. We have to remember that forgiveness is an act of our will, not a feeling that we conjure up.

Jesus says,

> But *to you who are listening* I say: *Love* your enemies, *do good* to those who hate you, *bless* those who curse you, *pray for* those who mistreat you. If someone slaps you on one cheek, *turn to them the other also*. If someone takes your coat, do not withhold your shirt from them. *Give to everyone* who asks you, and if anyone takes what belongs to you, *do not demand it back. Do to others as you would have them do to you.* (Luke 6:27–31)

Not everyone is "listening" to these critical words straight from the mouth of Jesus. *Love . . . do good . . . bless . . . pray for . . . turn the other cheek . . . give to everyone . . . don't demand stolen goods back . . . and do to others as you would have them do to you.* Jesus doesn't say to cancel those who hate you and get revenge on those who mistreat you. Nor to harbor unforgiveness toward those who slander you nor start campaigns to take down those who are against you. No, He says, "To you who are listening . . ." and many of us are not. We're cherry-picking Scripture to fit our lifestyle and narrative, hearing but not understanding, speaking but not listening.

I remember right where I was standing when I heard the Holy Spirit say, *Andi, turn the other cheek. Say nothing.* I was about to go into my hotel room after a speaking engagement and had been walking through some very personal, crippling opposition for a period of time. I was midthought about how I could use my words as weapons and write a passive-aggressive post that was indirectly aimed at the people who had hurt me, when the Holy Spirit interrupted my thoughts. I felt immediate conviction. I wanted to confess and talk it through with a close friend who would love me but give it to me straight. I picked up the phone to call her, and when I admitted what was stirring inside of me, including my morbid desire to share a passive-aggressive post that could get a lot of amens, she said, "Yeah . . . Don't do it. Whatever you'd write would come across like a subtweet." To which I asked, "What's a subtweet?" I mean, I'm on Twitter, but I'm not on Twitter, if you know what I mean. According to *Merriam-Webster*, a subtweet is "a usually mocking or critical tweet that alludes to another Twitter user without including a link to the user's account and often without directly mentioning the user's name."[4]

I heeded the words of the Holy Spirit to say nothing, as well as the advice from a friend, and instead cried out in prayer, intentionally blessing by name those who were cursing me.

Are we listening when the Holy Spirit nudges us to stand down and stay silent? Are we quick to listen, slow to speak, and slow to get angry (James 1:19), or are we hasty with the comebacks, swift to get angry, and horrible at listening? Are we sincerely willing to bless and pray for those who have wounded us, or do we eagerly call down fire upon them?

Ask yourself:

- Why do I need to say what I feel like I need to say? Wisdom, maturity, and emotional intelligence weigh where the other person is at, including their ability to engage in a helpful or unhelpful manner. So, ask yourself where you and the other party are at and if a conversation is necessary at this time.

- If I do indeed move forward and have a conversation, will they be able to hear what I am going to say?
- Am I trying to get this off my chest, or do I have a genuine desire to make amends?
- Am I offended or have I forgiven, and do I even need to speak to them about this if I have truly forgiven them? Step 9 in Celebrate Recovery says, "We made direct amends to such people whenever possible, except when to do so would injure them or others."[5] It can be unkind to have or send the "I've forgiven you for . . ." conversation, text, or email. If true forgiveness is there, it's not always necessary to let the other person know.
- Do I want to have this conversation for me, for them, for reconciliation, or to be right?

As I was getting ready one day, I found myself praying for my enemies. Yes, in my prayers, I did ask that they'd repent and see the error of their ways so they could walk with clean hands and a pure heart. As I prayed, I began to feel convicted, and my prayers shifted to, "Oh God . . . that *I'd* walk with clean hands and a pure heart! That I'd forgive and let go. That I'd remove the plank from my eye while trying to remove the speck from another's." Psalm 24:3–4 says,

> Who may ascend the mountain of the LORD?
> Who may stand in his holy place?
> The one who has *clean hands and a pure heart*,

who has not appealed to what is false,
and who has not sworn deceitfully. (CSB)

I want to stand in the presence of God with integrity, with nothing to prove and nothing to hide. I don't want to appeal to what is false and get caught up in conversations and situations that become derogatory and detrimental to the lives of others. I want to do the work to live with clean hands and a pure heart.

INTEGRITY IN HARD CONVERSATIONS

In a world where people are canceled in the court of public opinion, biblical integrity demonstrates a higher way. Whatever ending, change, or transition we're walking through, remember that others do not need to be thrown under the bus for us to walk in our purpose or calling. God is good and sovereign. Choosing integrity in change causes us to refuse to justify our choices before other people because we're simply living in obedience to God.

Matthew 18 is a rich chapter in its fullness, and within it, I'm going to zero in on dealing with sin and the cost of unforgiveness. Remember, integrity is "the quality of being honest and having strong moral principles; moral uprightness." Or "the state of being whole and undivided."[6]

When we're braving change, there are usually different forms of tension to manage, and a key tension is within our relationship to others.

Maybe you've been fired or let go or are changing roles or jobs. You could be moving to a new city or country, leaving all that you've known. And in these types of situations, as well as others not mentioned, if we feel wronged in any way, there can be a tendency to justify why we're doing what we're doing or explain away what's happened and why. In our conversations, we may even point out others' flaws and talk about how we perceive that they've mistreated us, whether it's true or untrue, and how we're morally upright in a certain scenario. We may post, text, or email passive-aggressively to appear honorable, but there is a higher way. If we truly believe we've been wronged by others or that sin is present in their lives, talking about it to someone other than the person we believe to be in sin or running a PR campaign to vindicate ourselves is not the biblical way.

> If your brother or sister sins, go and point out their fault, *just be-tween the two of you*. If they listen to you, you have won them over. But if they will not listen, *take one or two others along*, so that "every matter may be established by the testimony of two or three witnesses." If they still refuse to listen, *tell it to the church*; and if they refuse to listen even to the church, treat them as you would a pagan or a tax collector. (Matt. 18:15–17)

We often surrender to our human tendencies and "tell it to the church" before we talk "just between the two of us." We miss integral, biblical steps when we do this. The context of this passage has to do with confronting and dealing with sin in the church, so let us remember that gossip and slander are sins as well. To keep our integrity intact, may we choose not to cross the line of bearing false witness against another. It's a powerful choice to go to them first and have a brave conversation even if our voice shakes. If the accusation is true and what is taking place is sinful and they don't listen or repent, then take one or two others along to have a second conversation. Why does this progression matter? It's actually about giving restoration a chance because the God of Abraham, Isaac, and Jacob—the God of Israel—gave His people opportunities to repent and be restored time and time again. And then He sent Jesus once and for all, giving us the grace and mercy to repent and change. Therefore, when it comes to our brothers and sisters in Christ, we are charged to do the same. And listen, if they're unrepentant, refusing to listen, then you can "tell it to the church" and, as Jesus says, "treat them as you would a pagan or tax collector."

It's not lost on me that the next section of Matthew 18 has to do with unforgiveness. It's no surprise that when we believe the end justifies the means in conflict, instead of living with biblical integrity and having hard but good truth-in-love conversations, we begin to harbor unforgiveness in our hearts, believing the lie and playing a script over and over again that the world owes us something.

I love that after Jesus shares the model of healthy confrontation and restoration from sin with His disciples, Peter's hand shoots up with a question: "Lord, how many times shall I forgive my brother or sister who sins against me? Up to seven times?" (v. 21). This is a great question after the difficult task that Jesus has set before them. Even Peter is like, "Jesus, I have my limits. I'll do what you said, but exactly how many times do I have to forgive these fools?" And true to form, Jesus says, "I tell you, not seven times, but seventy-seven times" (v. 22). Ouch, Jesus. Why so many times? He then follows it up with a parable to illustrate God's mercy and our need to extend it to others.

In Matthew 18:21–35 we see the unmerciful servant who owes the king a debt that he cannot possibly pay. Due to the servant's inability to make things right, the king orders that the servant, his wife, and his children are all sold into slavery to repay the debt. The unmerciful servant falls to his knees and begs for the king's mercy, saying that he'll find a way to pay it back. The king takes pity on him and cancels all of his debts, letting him go to live a free life. But when the servant leaves the king's presence, he finds one of his fellow servants who owes him a debt of a hundred silver coins. He grabs him by the throat and begins to choke him, demanding that he pays what he owes. His fellow servant does the exact same thing the first servant did before the king, falling to his knees and begging for mercy, but unlike the king, the first servant refuses to forgive the debt and has the man thrown into prison. When the other servants see this, they go to the king and tell him how this man has acted after being forgiven so much. The king calls the man, rebukes him, and has him handed over to the jailers to be tortured until he's paid back all that he owes. Jesus goes on to say, "This is how my heavenly Father will treat each of you unless you forgive your brother or sister from your heart" (v. 35).

Both of these passages in Matthew 18 are reminders to us to keep our hands clean and our hearts pure—no matter the cost. I tend to remind myself that I will stand before God at the end of my life and give an account. There's a higher way, a narrow road, and it leads to life if we should choose to take it.

IT'S BIGGER THAN YOU THINK

Why does all of this even matter? Why do we need to recognize transition when we're in it and take the time to grieve, recover, and learn from all we've walked through? Why do we need to keep showing up in godly community and process endings and changes with integrity? Because there is a bigger play at hand. Souls are at stake. Generations are waiting to hear the testimony of the goodness of God in the land of the living.

Processing pain and grief with integrity gets us to the other side of life's major and minor transitions with our identity and honor still intact. Often, the battle to get to the other side isn't just about us, it's about countless others. It's bigger than you, *and* it's bigger than you think.

BUILDING ON THE ROCK

Scripture Meditation: Galatians 6:7–10

Do not be deceived: God cannot be mocked. A man reaps what he sows. Whoever sows to please their flesh, from the flesh will reap destruction; whoever sows to please the Spirit, from the Spirit will reap eternal life. Let us not become weary in doing good, for at the proper time we will reap a harvest if we do not give up. Therefore, as we have opportunity, let us do good to all people, especially to those who belong to the family of believers.

Take a moment and be still before God. Read the passage out loud. What stands out to you?

REFLECTION QUESTIONS

- How have you possibly not had integrity in endings, transition, or change? Have you lacked ownership of your side of the story? Have you avoided closure? Have you tried to control the narrative or outcomes that you have no power over? Have you avoided the principles in Matthew 18, and so on? Take some time before the Lord to confess and repent. Receive His grace, mercy, and forgiveness.
- Who do you need to forgive? Endings and change are hard, and the relational toll is real. Take some time to release people from the debt they owe you and place them back in the hands of God.

GUIDED PRAYER

Father, thank You that You're always with me. I ask that You would help me to process my grief, pain, endings, and transitions with integrity, even when I want to avoid them or blame others for all that I'm walking through. Please help me to see what is in my power to do to keep a tender heart. I pray that You'd give me wisdom and discernment to know the difference between healthy and unhealthy closure. Lead me on Your path of righteousness as I intentionally choose to surrender all on a daily basis. Empower me by Your Spirit to do good to all people, even when I'd rather not. May I listen to Your Spirit and obey Your Word as I choose to love my enemies, do good to those who hate me, and bless those who curse me. I repent of any revenge that I may have hidden in my heart, and I choose to walk on Your narrow road instead. Help me to have integrity in hard conversations and forgive (as an act of my will) seventy times seven. And remind me when I want to throw in the towel and be done with the mess of humanity that there's a bigger play at hand; eternity is at stake and the battle to get to the other side is worth it.

CHAPTER 8

CHOOSE GRATITUDE

Enter his gates with thanksgiving
   and his courts with praise;
   give thanks to him and praise his name.
For the LORD is good and his love endures forever;
   his faithfulness continues through all generations.

                              Psalm 100:4–5

Choosing gratitude in liminal spaces can be tricky to navigate as we find ourselves braving change. As humans, we crave stability and predictability, and a liminal space is anything but that. Marriage and family therapist Theodora Blanchfield says, "The word 'liminal' comes from the Latin word 'limen,' which means threshold. To be in a liminal space means to be on the precipice of something new but not quite there yet. You can be in a liminal space physically, emotionally, or metaphorically."[1]

When we had three kids under the age of three, Paul and I walked through one of the most difficult seasons of our lives. At that time, I was also struggling with postpartum depression. I felt heavily burdened in so many ways simultaneously. Memories from childhood around the abuse I suffered, as well as the difficult circumstances our family had walked through, came bubbling to the surface, causing me to question my sanity and in turn leading to a breakdown. This season was dark but also catalytic for my healing. As I look back, I think of how the relationships with my husband and children suffered the most as I figured out how to move through the pain. (I write a lot about how God helped me through this season in my book *She Is Free*.) Within this liminal space, I distinctly recall the choice we made to worship through it all. I'd turn up the music in the kitchen and dance with my baby girl on my hip and my playful toddlers at my feet. Every Sunday, I'd put on makeup, show up at church, and then cry it all off as I continued to praise in the midst of pain. When I look back on those memories, who I was, who we were, and what we walked through that transformed us to the core, it feels like a fever dream. Years later, we're not the same people. We have scars that tell a story of what felt like spiritual open-heart surgery, rehabilitation, and healing. And I know this: I'd be absolutely lost without God's rescuing and redeeming love. I'm completely undone if I sit in this reality for too long.

Grief and gratitude can go hand in hand. Choosing gratitude is a powerful force, but it doesn't erase the heartache and loss you may still feel. So, as we journey through this chapter, remember that there's room for the liminal space you may be in.

ENTER HIS GATES WITH THANKSGIVING

On January 23, 2021, I had a dream. I walked into a large auditorium that seated around three thousand people. I somehow innately knew this was our church in New York, and I was going to be teaching the Word that day. I could sense that the people were extremely weary. Weary from the toils of life, weary from 2020, and weary of one another. They were all spread out, yet quite a few people were there, and I remember being shocked that so many had shown up. There was a steady, peaceful hum as people milled around waiting for the service to begin.

I heard the Lord say to me, *Tell them, "Some of you say you can't feel or sense the presence of God. You've grown numb and cold to His presence. Psalm 100:4 says, 'I will enter his gates with* thanksgiving *in my heart, I will enter his courts with* praise.'" *Remind them that thanksgiving and praise usher them into My presence.*

In my dream, I knew that some of us had forgotten how to come to our gracious God with praise and thanksgiving. That we'd disregarded His goodness among the trials and allowed spiritual combat zones to sap us of our joy that is found in Him and Him alone.

I woke up convicted and went to Psalm 100:

A psalm. For giving grateful praise.

> Shout for joy to the LORD, all the earth.
>> Worship the LORD with *gladness*;
>> come before him with *joyful songs*.
> Know that the LORD is God.
>> It is he who made us, and *we are his*;
>> we are his people, the sheep of his pasture.
>
> Enter his gates with *thanksgiving*
>> and his courts with *praise*;
>> *give thanks to him and praise his name.*
> For the LORD is good and *his love endures forever*;
>> his faithfulness continues through all generations.

These words stand true throughout every generation and every moment that we have breath in our lungs. The more we give thanks, the more we become aware of His presence already operating and moving in our lives.

When I had this particular dream, our family was in the midst of our own change. Up until that point we'd been serving in New York City for just over eleven years, and in January of 2022, we transitioned the church to the next leaders to take it forward. Our assignment was beginning to shift, and many of the signs and factors I mentioned in chapter 2, "Recognize Transition When You're in It," were occurring in our lives. We were experiencing exhaustion of every imaginable kind, relationships were naturally changing, the gears were grinding, the grace was lifting, and the spiritual warfare and resistance seemed to be up close and unrelenting. I realized this dream was definitely a personal dream from God to remind me of my posture, but I believe it was also a word for the greater church.

In times of struggle or change, it's easy to lose sight of praise and thanksgiving because it's also necessary to lament and forge a pathway *through* the difficulty we're in the middle of. Seasons of simply existing and surviving must come to an end, yet even within such challenging moments in time, we must remember to give thanks for what we do have. Choosing gratitude in transition shifts our perspective and causes us to see clearly again.

From that time forward, I decided to make a slight but integral change to my prayer life. Instead of coming to God with my prayer list like we were having a work meeting, I established a new rhythm of beginning with gratitude. Now I sit down with my cup of hot coffee in the early hours before sunrise, visualizing His courts, and then open my mouth to simply say, "Good morning, God. Thank You for . . ." This simple practice can be a helpful aid to view life through a different lens, deliberately shifting a negative thought pattern we may be dwelling on and helping us to refocus and remember just how good, faithful, and present God is, no matter the trial or triumph we may be facing.

I love praying like this with an awareness that when Jesus breathed His last breath on the cross, the veil that separated us from the presence of God was torn in two so that all could have access to the throne room. After the ascension of Christ, we were given the gift of the Holy Spirit to be our Advocate (John 14:26), leading us to and reminding us of all truth. May we never take the privilege of His presence for granted!

THE THREE GS

I don't remember which child it was, and I don't even remember what they said, but I snapped.

We'd scrimped and saved enough money to go away on a fun summer vacation with our kids, and everything had been going fairly well until that morning. Apparently, everyone had woken up on the wrong side of the bed because the only sounds that fell out of the mouths of my babes were accompanied by a whiny and ungrateful tone. I had been teetering on the precipice of how much of the incessant sounds tantamount to nails on a chalkboard I could take, when I broke. We were at the pool enjoying the warm tropical breeze (well, trying to) when the final straw came down. I shot up, ripped off my hat and sunglasses to eyeball my children, and said, "That's enough! Look around. Do you even *see* the pool? The crystal-blue ocean? The peaceful, swaying palm trees? Oh, and these little drinks with maraschino cherries and cute paper umbrellas that we got for you? I've had enough." I quickly scrambled to grab all of my stuff and said to Paul, "I need a time-out." He smiled that smile that says, "I've got your back, baby. Get out of here and enjoy. Things are about to change." As I walked away, the whining ceased, and the low, slow, calming voice of my husband began to bring the kids in.

About an hour later, I came back to playful, happy children running up to me, genuinely apologizing for their lack of gratitude. The chair was open next to my husband, and he gave me that nod—the one that says, "It is finished."

I asked, "What on earth did you do?"

"Well," he said, "I instated 'the Three Gs.'"

"The three what?"

"The Three Gs: Be *grateful*, think on *good* things, and *go* with the flow."

We both smiled as we watched our kids splash and play in the pool, and from that day forward, "the Three Gs" have become a part of our family's culture. When things begin to turn upside down, or when one of us—parents included—feels entitled to something, or when we face loss or heartache, or if the atmosphere of the house gets whiny, ungrateful, or controlling, we remember the Three Gs, which is a choice to put ourselves in a simple posture of gratitude. When all I can seem to be aware of is what I don't have or what is difficult, I choose to be grateful for what I do have. When all I can focus on is what's wrong with the world, I take a deep breath and remember the goodness of God and all the things He has done and is continuing to do, whether I can see them with my eyes or not. First Chronicles 16:34 says, "Give thanks to the LORD, for he is good; his love endures forever." And when I think I can control others or particular outcomes, I choose to surrender, let go of anxiety, and go with the flow.

Humble yourselves, therefore, under God's mighty hand, that he may lift you up in due time. *Cast all your anxiety on him because he cares for you.*

Be alert and of sober mind. Your enemy the devil prowls around like a roaring lion looking for someone to devour. *Resist* him, *standing firm* in the faith, because you know that the family of believers throughout the world is undergoing the same kind of sufferings. (1 Pet. 5:6–9)

The verses that surround "Cast all your anxiety on him because he cares for you" are important for context because this chapter in 1 Peter is about those of us who are younger being charged to submit ourselves to godly authority. And in doing so we are charged to "clothe" ourselves in humility (Col. 3:12) with an understanding that God opposes the proud but gives grace and favor to the humble. Choosing to humble ourselves and submit to God causes us to put our worries and fears in the right place, on God, instead of carrying them like an endless burden or hoping someone else will take the load off us. It also reminds us to resist and stand firm. The devil will continue to prowl around, trying to steal whatever we'll let him have. Yet resisting him and standing firm in our faith in Christ our Rock, remembering that we're not alone in our struggle, helps us to go with God's flow and let go of control.

THE FIGHT FOR CHILDLIKE FAITH

The fight to remain childlike in our faith is a legitimate battle. In times of change, the enemy waits to sow seeds of offense and bitterness. When those seeds take root and grow, not only do they damage our personal life, but Hebrews 12:15 says the "bitter root grows up to cause trouble and defile many."

So, how does one remain childlike through difficulty? How do we dig out the seeds of pride and bitterness sown into our hearts and replace them with seeds that will bring life and not death? Jesus tells us how in Matthew 18:

> At that time the disciples came to Jesus and asked, "Who, then, is the greatest in the kingdom of heaven?"

He called a little child to him, and placed the child among them. And he said: *"Truly I tell you, unless you change and become like little children, you will never enter the kingdom of heaven.* Therefore, whoever takes the lowly position of this child is the greatest in the kingdom of heaven. And whoever welcomes one such child in my name welcomes me." (vv. 1–5)

Have you ever watched a child pick up a stick and enter an alternate universe, gallivanting around the backyard, speaking to an unseen foe, while endeavoring to take them down with their imaginary sword? What about listening to the vibrant, uninhibited stories of a child, pouring out of their mouth like colorful rainbows as they get lost in a world of wonder and make-believe? How about when you purchase an overpriced gift for your sweet, feisty three-year-old, but instead, they're obsessed with the box because their little body fits in it just so? You watch in awe as they're transported to a racetrack, zooming away at lightning speed, leaving the actual gift you got them by the wayside. Children are a wonder, and observing how they see the world gives me so much joy. Watching them discover the ordinary with curiosity and awe is a gift.

One of my favorite sounds on the planet is the innocent whisper of a child praying to God with untainted tenderness and an unguarded faith, believing that God really *can* do anything. My heart could burst watching children worship unhindered, oblivious of anyone else around them. Childlikeness and wonder-filled curiosity can ebb away the older we get unless we fight to cultivate them and remain in a state of awe. Jesus tells us that the Kingdom of Heaven belongs to such as these, so what does it look like, practically, for us to fight for our childlike faith in times of pain, loss, distress, and sorrow?

Trust. Leaning in with a posture of faith and assurance—even if things don't go the way we think or expect they should—that

God in His sovereignty knows the beginning from the end. He is with us, and He is always for us.

I heard the Holy Spirit whisper to me, *Do you trust Me?* to which I side-eyed the heavens and said, "Yeeesss?" I was staying at my parents' place in California at the time, getting ready for the day and praying in the shower, when I had a flash-forward vision of what was about to go down in our lives, and it shook me to the core. We were about to lose some things that at the time we believed to have been a promise for our future. To those around us, it may have looked like we lost everything, but God showed me that it was actually His mercy and protection. Did I trust Him? *Yeeesss?* To the extent that I knew I could while resisting the urge to figure out how to run an undignified, self-preserving PR campaign to try and explain to the world what was happening and why.

I've had so many moments in life just like this . . . where the Holy Spirit nudges me with His still small voice, *Do you trust Me?* while I twitch, knowing that if I choose trust, it will most likely be followed by a choice to humble myself, stay tender, and remain still while God does what He needs to do in the soil of my heart. This is the only way I know to stay childlike in my faith. By choosing to lay down my ego, do the hard heart work, hold my tongue, and yield once again. A "have your way" posture that trusts like a child who has confidence that their mother or father will put food on the table at the end of the day.

We're all painfully aware that there will be endless opportunities to be offended and to harden our hearts, but Jesus tells us, "Unless *you* change and become like little children, you will never enter the kingdom of heaven" (Matt. 18:3). The commitment to stay tenderhearted is on us. The transformation comes in how we respond to life's challenges and changes. Think of how an innocent child with a secure attachment responds to correction or love with purity and innocence. When that secure attachment to a parent or caregiver is present, they feel comfortable, comforted, safe, and protected, even in discipline. Our attachment to God is trustworthy and secure, so His love or discipline is always for our good.

Knowing this to be true, can we thank God not just in the good things but in the hard things too? Can we remember that He is King and the center of the story, whatever the circumstances may be? Can we remain faithful while we wait, remembering that nothing is wasted?

Romans 8:25–28 says,

> But if we hope for what we do not yet have, we wait for it patiently.
>
> In the same way, the Spirit helps us in our weakness. We do not know what we ought to pray for, but the Spirit himself intercedes for us through wordless groans. And he who searches our hearts knows the mind of the Spirit, because the Spirit intercedes for God's people in accordance with the will of God.
>
> *And we know that in all things God works for the good of those who love him, who have been called according to his purpose.*

We've heard it, we've quoted it, we've reminded ourselves of it: "He works all things together for our good," but when hope is deferred, our hearts tend to grow sick, tired, and calloused. Oh, but when a longing is realized and bursts forth in our life like a fruitful tree in season—laden with life and fulfillment—it gives reassurance to those still waiting in the valley (see Prov. 13:12). There is no fear when the wicked succeed and no need to vindicate ourselves when trust is at the center of our relationship with God.

Psalm 37 is a psalm of childlike trust and assurance in God:

> *Trust* in the LORD and do good;
>   dwell in the land and enjoy safe pasture.

> *Take delight* in the LORD,
> and he will give you the desires of your heart.
>
> *Commit* your way to the LORD;
> *trust in him* and he will do this:
> He will make your righteous reward shine like the dawn,
> your vindication like the noonday sun.
>
> *Be still* before the LORD
> and wait patiently for him;
> do not fret when people succeed in their ways,
> when they carry out their wicked schemes.
>
> *Refrain from anger* and turn from wrath;
> *do not fret*—it leads only to evil.
> For those who are evil will be destroyed,
> but those who *hope in the LORD* will inherit the land.
> (vv. 3–9)

The attributes we see in this psalm will keep our hearts in a state of childlikeness: trusting in God, taking delight in Him, committing our way to Him, being still before Him, refraining from anger, not fretting, and hoping in the Lord . . .

I urge you, stay tender and blameless at all costs. The Kingdom of Heaven belongs to those with faith like a child.

REMEMBER AND CELEBRATE

Remember who you are and how far you've come. But even more so, remember who He is and what He's done.

Take a moment to think about what you've overcome. Have you acknowledged the reality that you're still here and you still love Jesus? Can you recall the times that you didn't let offense or bitterness take over, even though contending for a soft heart felt like an unwinnable battle? What choices have you made that have propelled you in the right direction, down the narrow road? Think back to your choice to worship in the face of loss and how it kept you on a firm foundation. Reflect on the periods of time when you struggled to make choices that would preserve your integrity. You've done it before, and you can do it again.

I'm unreasonably hard on myself. I have a specific memory of sitting with my husband one evening while the kids were tucked into bed. I was giving myself yet another browbeating for not measuring up to the impossible standard I had set for myself when he said, "You may not be where you want to be, but you're not where you used to be." Touché.

It's easy to replay pain or rehearse the mistakes we've made and live in regret. From friendship to leadership, parenting, and marriage—for me the list can be never-ending. But what if we chose to remember the good things as well, not just the sorrow and hurt? We've established the need to grieve and be kind to ourselves to get to a place of acceptance, but what narrative or script are we ruminating on as we process through the present transition, loss, or change we're in? Humans are meaning makers, and when we're not diligent in bringing our every thought and motive before God, we'll start to make up "meaning," assigning motive to others, once again bearing false witness in our hearts. And when we're unguarded, we'll speak it out to others. Don't do it! Slowly back away from this particular pitfall and ask God to show you the truth through the lens of the gospel, not your struggle. You'll be amazed at His liberating love and perspective.

So, as we remember how far we've come and how faithful our God is, let's also remember to celebrate the wins and gain wisdom from the losses.

Do you know how to celebrate? I mean like get out the confetti, balloons, streamers, and party hats? Turn the music way up and lose yourself in it?

Growing up, we weren't rich by any stretch of the imagination. My parents worked hard to provide for us, pay the bills, and sometimes just make ends meet. I never worried, but I also knew we didn't live in a mansion on a hill. We lived in a little blue-gray house by the train tracks in a lower-income neighborhood, and some of my best childhood memories were created in that space.

Every birthday, my mom went all out to make us feel special. I look back with affection at the pictures and the memories I can recall from my fifth birthday in particular. She had made me a pink cake in the shape of the number 5 with cute little bees and beehives thoughtfully placed on top of it. Balloons hung upside down from the ceiling, and streamers were strung all around me. And my dress . . . I loved that thing. My mom had sown it for me. It was this beautiful dusty rose color with tiny flowers all over it. The sleeves jutted out like miniature wings ready to take flight, and the ribbons running up and down the front were the perfect embellishment. I always felt like a princess on my birthday. I knew that I was loved and celebrated for who I was.

My mom has reflected to me how much she enjoyed doing all she could for our birthdays. She told me that she'd imagine herself as a child and ask, "What would be fun? What would be a really good surprise?" She desired that each of her kids were, in her words, "seen, loved, and cherished"—and we were. Whether we had abundance or were in need, we celebrated.

Remembering how far we've come is worth celebrating. Remembering how good God is reminds us that He is worthy of *all* of our praise and thanksgiving. Pausing to glory in His kindness makes us aware of His presence. Remembering and celebrating keep us in a continual posture of gratitude. What can you remember and celebrate today?

WORSHIP ANYWAY

I have found that heartbreak can give voice to healing and hope. This makes no sense except for the divine, unfathomable truth that our God, the Living Word, put on flesh and entered into our despair to redeem with His perfect love all that had been lost.

When my mom told me the story of how "It Is Well with My Soul" was written, I sat there with her and wept.

In 1871, a man by the name of Horatio G. Spafford had been living a good life in Chicago with his wife, Anna, and their four daughters. At the time, Spafford was a successful lawyer and real estate investor, as well as an elder in his Presbyterian church. They were friends with and supporters of the evangelist Dwight L. Moody. That year, tragedy struck when the Great Chicago Fire ravaged the city October 8–10. At least three hundred people perished, around one hundred thousand were left homeless, and $200 million worth of property was destroyed, including Spafford's real estate investments and law firm.

By 1873, Spafford was concerned about Anna's health and decided to send his family on vacation to England where they would also be attending revival services held by Moody. When their finances took another hit by the Panic of 1873, Spafford was detained by last-minute business concerns, so he sent his wife and four daughters, aged eleven, nine, five, and two, on the French steamship *Ville du Havre* ahead of him. One week into the trip, the *Ville du Havre* collided with the iron-hulled Scottish ship *Loch Earn*, snapping the French ship in half.

Anna woke her daughters and took them onto the deck as she cried out to God to either save them or make them willing to die. Within twelve minutes, the ship sank into the icy waters of the Atlantic, taking the lives of 226 of the 313 souls on the *Ville du Havre*, including Horatio and Anna's four daughters. Anna was found clinging to a piece of the wreckage, rescued, and taken to Cardiff, Wales, where she penned a telegraph, sent by the Western Union Telegraph Company to Spafford, that said, "Saved alone. What shall I do?"

Spafford immediately left Chicago to meet his wife in Liverpool. As he crossed the Atlantic, the captain called Spafford to his cabin at one point and told him that, to the best of his recollection, they were over the place where his daughters had perished.

According to one of Spafford's daughters born after the tragedy, her father wrote some of "It Is Well with My Soul" while on this journey.

> When peace like a river attendeth my way,
> When sorrows like sea billows roll;
> Whatever my lot, Thou hast taught me to say,
> It is well, it is well with my soul.
> Chorus:
> It is well with my soul,
> It is well, it is well with my soul.[2]

In 1876, Ira Sankey, a known gospel singer associated with Dwight L. Moody, stayed in Horatio and Anna's home for a couple of weeks. According to Sankey, this was when all of the words to the hymn were written in commemoration of the death of the Spaffords' four daughters. The music for the hymn was composed by Phillip P. Bliss and officially published by Bliss and Sankey. It was first sung by Bliss before a large gathering hosted by Moody on November 4, 1876.

Heartbreakingly, these events were not the end of the Spaffords' sorrows. A son, Horatio Gates Spafford II, was born to them in 1877, but he died of scarlet fever before he turned five. However, the Spaffords had two more daughters, Bertha and Grace, born in 1878 and 1881. "It Is Well with My Soul" is a "worship anyway" sort of song. The Spaffords' heartbreak gave voice to healing and hope to countless generations who still sing the words, "It is well with my soul."

This story is a harrowing reminder to us that, whatever losses we have suffered, whatever endings or changes we have walked through, we may choose to lift up our weary heads and worship anyway. As we command our souls to sing, declaring in faith, "It is well," may we become cognizant of the goodness of God and recover and heal from the heartbreak while regaining the strength to find joy again as gratitude willingly spills out of our mouths. Remember, grief and gratitude can go hand in hand: choosing gratitude is a powerful force, but it doesn't erase the heartache and loss you may still feel.

BUILDING ON THE ROCK

Scripture Meditation: Psalm 37:3–9

> Trust in the LORD and do good;
>> dwell in the land and enjoy safe pasture.
> Take delight in the LORD,
>> and he will give you the desires of your heart.
>
> Commit your way to the LORD;
>> trust in him and he will do this:
> He will make your righteous reward shine like the dawn,
>> your vindication like the noonday sun.
>
> Be still before the LORD
>> and wait patiently for him;
> do not fret when people succeed in their ways,
>> when they carry out their wicked schemes.

Refrain from anger and turn from wrath;
  do not fret—it leads only to evil.
For those who are evil will be destroyed,
  but those who hope in the LORD will inherit the land.

What (and whom) are you trusting in? Delighting in? What (and whom) are you committing your way to? Are you able to simply be still before God and refrain from anger? Can you make the conscious choice to "not fret"? Where (and in what) have you placed your hope? Take some time to reflect on this Scripture. Be honest with your answers before God. Repent, delight, hope, trust, be still . . .

REFLECTION QUESTIONS

- The cultivation of gratitude takes intention. In what ways do you need to shift your prayer life from one of a transactional list, to one beginning with thanksgiving and praise?
- How can you produce and multiply childlikeness in your life?

GUIDED PRAYER

Father, I'm in awe of Your steadfast love. I come to You with thanksgiving in my heart, and I enter Your courts with praise on my lips! I have breath in my lungs to shout of Your goodness for all of my days. You are a righteous God who knows the beginning from the end, and I lay my heart down once again to trust in You with everything that I am. You are faithful, even when I am faithless and broken. You are just when I am dishonest with myself and others. You never leave me or forsake me when I turn my back and live life my own way. Father, forgive me for the times I've placed myself at the center of the story and tried to make myself god. You are King of Kings and Lord of Lords forevermore. Heal the broken and bitter places of my heart that have robbed me of tenderness and childlikeness. Show me where to repent, receive Your love, and worship anyway, proclaiming, "It is well with my soul," even when my circumstances say the opposite. Whatever happens, and in every circumstance, You are worthy of all my praise.

CHAPTER 9

CHOOSE RHYTHMS OF REST

If the devil cannot make us bad, he will make us busy.

Corrie ten Boom

On Saturday mornings, as the sun rises over the towering oak trees outside our bedroom window, the warmth kisses my face like a gentle alarm clock, inviting me to sit up and take joy in the glory of our Creator. We're not the "black out the windows and turn on the white noise" sort of sleepers. When we're tired, we sleep, and on our day of rest, it's a simple pleasure to have the sunrise slowly wake us before we shuffle downstairs to get our first cup of coffee.

Most Saturdays, I'll sit in my bed for hours drinking coffee, journaling, reading, resting, and then reading some more until our children wake up. Most weeks, after we're all up, I'll fill the house with the smell of bacon and whatever else we decide sounds good for that unhurried Saturday. Usually eggs, maybe pancakes, avocado, berries, a small green salad, sourdough toast—all the things. Around the brunch table, we decide what we'd like to do that day. Sometimes we spend it all together, other times we split up, but whatever we do, we slow down, release any notion that we *should* do anything, and take satisfaction in simply going with the flow and enjoying one another.

This tends to be our family's day to Sabbath, rest, and delight in our God, His creation, and one another. The to-do list is set aside as we choose to rest from our work.

John Mark Comer says, "The Hebrew word Shabbat means 'to stop.' But it can also be translated 'to delight.' It has this dual idea of stopping and also of joying in God and our lives in his world. The Sabbath is an entire day set aside to follow God's example, to stop and delight."[1] When we're in the midst of change, it's easy to forget to "stop and delight" in God and His creation because there's so much to do or, quite honestly, worry about. Whether you're packing up a house to move or tying up loose ends in the workplace to step into what's next, it's easy to get overwhelmed by the checklist. But to cease from work and choose to dwell in God's goodness in the middle of transition is to have a posture of surrender, trusting that God is fully aware of every detail and leading you in the right direction.

What we behold, we become. When we pause to behold our Creator and King, our way of looking at our circumstances becomes gospel-centered instead of *us*-centered. To find a rhythm of rest is a choice. Just remember, there will always be too much to do; even when we clear out our inbox or check that last box on our to-do list, fresh emails will sneak in and populate that clean, empty space, and new tasks will happily present themselves.

IS THE SABBATH REST FOR TODAY?

"How are you doing with the commandment, 'You shall not murder'?"

Paul and I looked at each other and nervously tried not to laugh. "I mean, good. Ten out of ten."

"What about keeping the Sabbath day holy?"

We sat silent for a moment, pondering the question. "Probably more like five, maybe six, out of ten?"

Joe, our soul-care counselor, paused and let what we'd said sink in.

Although God does not require us to live by Israel's laws any longer, the invitation to enter into Sabbath rest remains. This conversation with Joe made me realize that we unwittingly presume that only a few of the commandments are obvious, applicable wisdom for today, like thou shall not murder, commit adultery, or steal, but we treat a few of the other commandments as circumstantial, like thou shall not bear false witness, covet, make idols, or take the Lord's name in vain, and honor your father and mother. But Sabbath? That one was for way back when. That's Old Testament. God understands that I have too much to do. Right?

Maybe you're asking questions like I did: "But *is* the Sabbath for the New Testament believer, especially if we don't live by the laws of the Old Testament any longer? Did Jesus keep the Sabbath holy, and if He did, how do we follow suit as His disciples?" Immediately, my mind went to a few different stories, like how Jesus's disciples were hungry, so they began to pick the heads of grain from the grain fields to eat them on the Sabbath (Matt. 12:1–2), and how Jesus healed a man with a shriveled hand on the Sabbath (vv. 9–14), not to mention delivered a demon-possessed man (vv. 22–23), upsetting the Pharisees and, according to them, not keeping the Sabbath day holy, which caused them to conspire against him (v. 14). In the middle of this wild Sabbath day, Jesus says, "For the Son of Man is Lord of the Sabbath" (v. 8).

What does this mean, and what are the implications for us as followers of Jesus?

Historically, God established a rhythm of rest at the very beginning of Scripture, in Genesis 2:2–3: "By the seventh day *God completed His work* which He had done, and *He rested on the seventh day from all His work* which He had done. Then God blessed the seventh day and sanctified it, because on it *He rested from all His work* which God had created and made" (NASB). Right after God establishes a pattern of work for six days and rest, or "Shabbat," on the seventh day, He creates humans and places them in the garden of Eden to *dwell* with Him. We then see in the account of the fall in Genesis 3, from the very beginning, humanity rebels and turns to itself as god. Further into the Old Testament, from the tabernacle in the wilderness to the temple in Jerusalem, we see time and again that God's people consistently disregard His design, from not worshiping idols all the way to keeping the Sabbath day holy. He longs to abide with His people in trust and intimacy, but over and over again, humankind rejects His perfect plan.

But then God's presence came to dwell among us in and through the life of Jesus.

And the Word became flesh and dwelt among us, and we have seen his glory, glory as of the only Son from the Father, *full of grace and truth*. (John bore witness about him, and cried out, "This was he of whom I said, 'He who comes after me ranks before me, because he was before me.'") *For from his fullness we have all received, grace upon grace. For the law was given through Moses; grace and truth came through Jesus Christ.* (John 1:14–17 ESV)

God's presence came to dwell with us through the person of Jesus! This wild grace that we've been given, even when we reject God's plan, is too immeasurable to comprehend. The law was given through Moses so that God's people would turn to, obey, dwell with, and rest in Him, but after they failed repeatedly, Christ came to give us grace.

Jesus, being both God and man, completely understood the heart of the Sabbath.

In Matthew 11, Jesus says, "Come to me, all you who are weary and burdened, and *I will give you rest*. Take my yoke upon you and learn from me, for I am gentle and humble in heart, and you will find rest for your souls" (vv. 28–29). Jesus has the ability to *give us rest*. For Israel, the weight of the law had become too burdensome to carry—and today, without Jesus, I would say it's the same. These words were and are revolutionary. So in Matthew 12, when we see Jesus seemingly blowing Sabbath out of the water by healing two different people as well as walking with His disciples as they gathered food—which according to the law were forbidden at the time—and subsequently proclaiming that He is "Lord of the Sabbath," we have to stop and ask, Does this mean we don't need to Sabbath any longer, because Jesus did work on the Sabbath and is "Lord of the Sabbath"?

Simply put, Jesus is the fulfillment of the promise. He *is* God's rest come to dwell among us here on earth. And before His death, resurrection, and ascension, Jesus promised us the gift of the Holy Spirit: "All this I have spoken while still with you. But the Advocate, *the Holy Spirit, whom the Father will send in my name*, will teach you all things and will remind you of everything I have said to you" (John 14:25–26). The Father sends the Holy Spirit in Jesus's name later, in Acts 2, instituting the renewal of all creation through the promised Messiah. The invitation to come before Jesus in Sabbath rest remains, and as we respond to this invitation, we accomplish God's original plan for us to cease from hard and heavy work and dwell in perfect intimacy with God's presence. We have been given the precious gift of the Holy Spirit to be our Advocate who teaches us and reminds us of everything that Jesus has taught us through the Holy Scriptures.

In an article for the BibleProject, Missy Takano, a missionary with TeachBeyond, writes,

> Jesus reminds the people of God's original intention for the Sabbath: unity with God, creation, and each other. Jesus teaches that the Sabbath points to him, the one Israel's prophets promised would come to mercifully restore the rhythm of all creation.
>
> When followers of Jesus observe the Sabbath, we live as if this restoration has already taken place. We take a break from the broken rhythms of hustle and hardship to set aside a time to honor Jesus' rule, enjoy his presence, and extend rest to the world around us. When we trust God's invitation to come to him and truly rest, we become places where his presence can dwell.[2]

Choosing to enter into and honor the Sabbath is a move of surrender and trust. In case we forget, the very first commandment is "You shall have no other gods before me" (Exod. 20:3), and that includes ourselves. When we place ourselves at the center of the story, we become gods, determined by what we can accomplish rather than resting in who God is.

THE PRACTICALITIES

How do we slow down the crazy and work from a place of energized rest instead of rushing to the weekend to finally rest from all of our work?

At a retreat with other pastors and business leaders, my husband heard Greg Surratt, the founding pastor of Seacoast Church, quote Rick Warren saying that the way to find a rhythm of rest is to "divert daily, withdraw weekly, (court quarterly), and abandon annually." Greg added in "court quarterly" for the married people out there. Even though it messes up the almost perfect flow of alliteration here, I'm also going to add in, "date weekly."

What does it look like to "divert daily" and do things that have nothing to do with work? What can we implement in our day-to-day that relaxes and refreshes us? I'm a morning person, so I tend to get up before my household, pour a cup of coffee, and take some time to read the Bible, walk around the living room, and pray, journal, or read a good discipleship book. I also genuinely enjoy working out as many times per week as I can, as I find it's good for me, spirit, mind, and body. If I can't get to a class at the gym, I'll take the dog on a long walk in the sunshine, pray, and do a quick workout or stretches when I get home. I also love a good story, so getting lost in a novel or watching a show or movie with the family is always at the top of the list. Connection to one another refuels us, so we try to have dinner around the table as many nights per week as possible, followed by a good board game when we're all in the mood.

One thing that helps me "divert daily" is scheduling in margin. Anxiety sinks into my gut when I place too many things back-to-back in my calendar. If you can, plan for margin, understanding that there will absolutely be some days when the margin flies right out the window.

How can you "divert daily"?

_____

_____

_____

_____

"Withdrawing weekly" refers to our weekly Sabbath rest. As I mentioned at the start of this chapter, sleeping in, having a long, drawn-out time to read and reflect, making a good meal, taking our time to eat it while connecting, and afterward, choosing to do only what causes us to delight in God, one another, and His creation is our Sabbath rhythm. If Sunday is your Sabbath, a slow start followed by worship at your local church and family lunch or dinner with friends could be what brings you joy. Maybe it's a walk on the beach or a hike in the mountains, turning your phone to Airplane Mode to abandon all technology. It could be the simple pleasure of cooking a good meal from scratch because the rest of the week is so hectic you can barely scrape dinner together to feed the troops. Maybe you glory in organization and love to have a good purge from time to time. Do you love to tend a garden or take care of your house plants? Maybe having no plans is the plan: legitimate physical rest, giving yourself the option to catnap all day in your pajamas without any guilt. It's possible you love to slowly walk down each aisle of the grocery store like I do, *alone*, deciding what would be fun to eat for the week. It could be a meal with friends, sunbathing on the beach or in your backyard, surfing, skiing, shopping, going for an extended run, going to the movies and getting that popcorn with extra butter and peanut M&M's—whatever it is, cease from work and delight in God, His creation, and those in your midst.

How can you "withdraw weekly"?

_____

_____

_____

_____

To "date weekly," or biweekly, is fundamental. Before Paul and I were engaged, married, and then doing life with our four children, we naturally found a cadence of dating weekly. Even in our early twenties, as we were getting to know one another, we were extremely busy people with plenty of excuses not to get time together. I can remember my husband's intentionality within our first month of dating. We went out once a week, and I can recall all four dates: Our first movie date was *Moulin Rouge*, followed up the next week with my inaugural experience of eating Thai food in Newton (Sydney, Australia). The following week, fresh seafood at Nick's in Darling Harbour, and the week after that, we ate at Café Sydney. Six months later, we got engaged, and six months after that, we got married, and Paul has continued to purposefully put date night first. When we had Zeke, our firstborn, after having him home for only a couple of days, my mom kicked us out and told us to go and get a coffee together. She said it was important that we established, or reestablished, dating one another when kids came into the picture. I cried as I walked out the door, feeling like I was abandoning my firstborn son, as she smiled and assured me he'd be fine for an hour. I laugh now at what I perceived to be my then-bossy mother, but she was right: Putting date night in place before we were married changed our lives. My husband still sends me weekly calendar invites for our date nights, prioritizing our connection. I will say this: Date nights don't have to cost anything. A picnic at a local park or taking a drive to watch the sunset together are totally free.

A close friend who happened to be single at the time that I wrote this book penned these words in a message to me:

As an individual in their single season, the relationship I'm focused on deepening and keeping the "spark" alive with is Jesus. If I can't maintain my relationship with Jesus, how in the world do I expect to maintain my relationship with my future spouse? This is a season of practicing emotional intimacy and we do that with Jesus. We get to master emotional intimacy without the messiness of physical intimacy. That way when we do start dating someone, we understand intimacy as more than just a physical act.

As singles, we can't just wait around for someone to sweep us off our feet out of nowhere. We can practice and implement the rhythm of dating weekly/biweekly into our routines now. It's wise to practice intimacy with Jesus in this season, so that once we enter into a marriage, we will have a better understanding of intimacy with our spouse.

How can you "date weekly"?

_____

_____

_____

_____

Now to "court quarterly." If you're single, find a time once every three months to get out on your own and dream with God. If you're married and have the ability to get away overnight or even longer, put it in the calendar before everything else fills it up. To this day, we tell our kids when they ask us why we're going away *again*, "We're just leaving to fall more in love with one another." They always smile and act grossed out, but we know that over the years it has built security and safety in our home. Whether you're single or married, this doesn't have to be a weekend away but could be a full day out without distraction once a quarter to dream with God.

How can you "court quarterly"?

_____

_____

_____

_____

And finally, "abandon annually." Once a year, take time away, either on your own or with your family, spouse, or friends. I have distinct memories from childhood of our family crossing the border from Washington State into Coeur d'Alene, Idaho, to stay at either the Ramada Inn, Motel 6, or its budget-friendly equivalent because it had a pool. We spent hours in the sun, soaking the exorbitant amounts of chlorine into our skin, and when we needed a change of scenery, we'd go over to Coeur d'Alene Lake and eat our potato chips and soggy tuna sandwiches, usually with the chips shoved between the bread as well. It didn't cost much, but the memory still brings me joy. Whether you get away once a year to an extravagant location or a simple place of rest and recovery on a tight budget, plan and carve out the time before the cares of this world shout louder, compete for your attention, and fill up your calendar.

How (and where) can you "abandon annually"?

_____

_____

_____

_____

These are merely suggestions. Take what works for you and your natural flow and implement it, or simply leave it. You know your life and what you need.

THE GOOD SHEPHERD

One of the wallpaper options on my iPhone is a picture of the Arkansas River at sunset in Buena Vista, Colorado. The clouds bear a resemblance to pink cotton candy, causing the riverbed rocks to take on a burnt orange hue while the rippling river does what it does and rushes on by. Just looking at this particular wallpaper, it's like I can hear, smell, and even feel this sacred place in my bones. When I took this specific picture, I was at the halfway point of spending two weeks in a counseling intensive. In this time of "abandoning annually" with the intention to release the past and welcome growth, Psalm 23 took on a new layer of meaning in my life.

> The LORD is my shepherd, *I lack nothing.*
> *He makes me* lie down in green pastures,
> *he leads me* beside quiet waters,
> *he refreshes* my soul.
> *He guides me* along the right paths
> for his name's sake. (vv. 1–3)

These first few verses materialized as I read them by the river. The actual reality that I lack nothing in Him is a lifelong revelation I plan to pursue and rest in. The progression of "He makes me, leads me, refreshes me, and guides me," points toward how *He* helps us find true rest in Him and Him alone.

We all know that with the gift of our free will, God doesn't actually *make us* do anything. But a life submitted to Christ longs to be led to pleasant and secure places. So, if the Good Shepherd wants to *make us* lie down in green pastures, why wouldn't we follow His lead instead of wearing *busy* as a badge of honor? Anywhere He leads us is trustworthy, and even just a moment beside quiet waters goes deep down into our very being. His tender and powerful presence refreshes our soul as we remember that He guides us along the right paths for *His* name's sake, not our own. Can we truly surrender and trust where the Good Shepherd is leading us?

Say this with me:

- I lack nothing with the Lord as my Shepherd.
- He makes me lie down and find rest in Him.
- He leads me beside quiet waters to safe and pleasant places.
- He refreshes my soul in ways that no earthly relationship or possession ever could.
- He guides me along the right paths to bring glory to His name, not my own.

Do you see who the center of the story is? It's the Good Shepherd. And the rest of the psalm is equally as powerful.

> Even though I walk
>> through the darkest valley,
> *I will fear no evil,*
>> for you are with me;
> your rod and your staff,
>> they comfort me.
>
> *You prepare a table before me*
>> in the presence of my enemies.

177

You anoint my head with oil;
   my cup overflows.
Surely your goodness and love will follow me
   all the days of my life,
and *I will dwell in the house of the* LORD
   forever. (vv. 4–6)

For me, this psalm shows us a vast picture of life, as an "all the days of my life" sort of psalm. There will be seasons of rest and renewal, seasons of darkness and difficulty, as well as moments of favor and overflow. Our days on this earth are nuanced, wild, and wonderful.

In the darkest night(s) of my soul, God continues to remind me that *His* perfect love has the ability to cast out fear as I am perfected in His love. When I operate from a place of agreement with fear in the midst of pain and difficulty, I can choose to see it as an opportunity to re-center myself in Christ and be perfected in love instead of catastrophizing or being hard on myself. Remember that 1 John 4:18 tells us, "Fear has to do with punishment," so ask yourself why you think you deserve to be punished rather than receive perfect love. I believe the truth you hear from the Holy Spirit and understand from this Scripture will set you free.

I remember a specific time when God gave me a visual picture of Psalm 23. In my mind's eye, I saw myself at a large table. At each head of the table sat the Father and the Son, and across from me was the Person of the Holy Spirit. The table was laden with some of the richest foods I've ever seen in my life. As I looked up, I saw stadium seating surrounding us that was filled with dark and evil spirits. I looked to the Father and asked, "Why did you invite my enemies here?" to which He replied, "So they would know who your Father is. It is I who anoints you, provides for you, protects you, and causes your cup to overflow." This picture has stuck with me every time I have read Psalm 23, leading me to a place where I understand that His goodness and love will follow me for the rest of my life. Psalm 23 is also a point at which the psalmist commits to dwell in the house of the Lord all the days of his life. With a God so good, so gracious to give us rest, walk with us in utter darkness, and anoint us, provide for us, and protect us, a natural response is to dwell in His courts.

As we brave the changes in front of us, remember, there is no need to justify our rest. We're usually the last person we take care of, and when we do, we feel guilt for "doing nothing." It's a simple invitation that we can say yes or no to. And when we say yes to entering into rest, we're creating healthy boundaries as we say no to the things that drain us and only withdraw from our lives.

THE MINISTRY OF PRESENCE

Sabbath rest causes us to be present in the moment, acknowledging the eternal while savoring the presence of God, cognizant that the Kingdom of Heaven is at hand.

If you struggle to be present, just know that you're not alone. Remember the quote at the start of this chapter by Corrie ten Boom, "If the devil cannot make us bad, he will make us busy"? It's easy to allow distraction to be lord and king of our lives in the world we live in. We carry a tiny computer in the form of a phone with us everywhere we go. It encompasses so much of our daily life. We can access information for just about anything, purchase a product at the tap of our finger, call, email, text, and generally connect with the world around us within seconds. We schedule our lives, entertain ourselves with every app imaginable, and in doing so, have the ability to completely tune out what's going on around us. We know technology isn't going anywhere, so choosing whether it holds us or we hold it is important, unless we're going to live off the grid. And it's not just with our phones, is it? We've been trained not to really hear one another, to sit in a conversation simply to listen and practice the ministry of presence. We're usually ready with advice or platitudes that may or may not help the other person in the scenario. Sometimes people simply need to be seen and heard.

So here are a few thoughts on how you can practice the ministry of presence:

- When you sit at a table with others, especially over a meal, try putting your phone in your bag or pocket—or even better, somewhere away from you so you're not tempted to take it out and check it. We have a "no phones at the table" rule in our house, whether we're out to eat or having breakfast, lunch, or dinner at home.
- On your chosen Sabbath day, try putting your phone on Do Not Disturb or Airplane Mode for twenty-four hours and see how you do. Making this a practice is a game changer.
- When someone you know calls out of the blue or asks if you have time to talk, being able to say, "This is not a good time because I can't give you my full attention. Let's schedule a time so I can be fully present with you," is a great way to practice being present.
- Read the moment. Know if someone needs you to just listen and not respond.

How can you personally practice the ministry of presence?

_____

_____

FIGHT THE RIGHT BATTLES

"What hill would you absolutely die on?"

We were sitting with two friends after dinner, all curled up on the couch, when one of them asked this question. We went around, answering with the "hill" we were willing to die on, or the fight we were willing to fight.

When it got to Paul, he had a contemplative look on his face, unsure of how to answer. He looked at me and said, "I wonder what hill I would die on." I paused, then said, "You'd die on everyone else's hill for them." Without a doubt, one of my husband's absolute strengths is believing in and fighting for others. And it's also his weakness when he does these things for others more than they're willing to do them for themselves. He loves people, but if he's not careful, it sneaks into the territory of enabling, producing entitlement in those who are being enabled. And what's the outcome of that? In the past, it's caused him to be spread thin, distracted, overwhelmed, and stressed instead of putting the best of his energy into taking care of first things first.

So, why does this matter, especially in the context of rest? The hill we're willing to die on speaks to passion—what we're willing and unwilling to fight for. Are you willing to make room for rest in your life? Would you die on that hill?

There will always be so much to do, but will we put the oxygen mask on ourselves before we take care of everyone else around us? We can't fight everyone else's battles and be absorbed in things that aren't ours to fix or carry. On the simplest of levels, we can't accomplish our day-to-day without establishing a pattern of rest. From adolescence to adulthood, having different demands such as study and/or work expectations, to being single, engaged, and married, having kids and then an empty nest, let your season inform you as you find your rhythm of grace.

REST AND RECOVER BEFORE BUILDING

"Be kind to yourself" are words that my husband and I often say to one another.

Have you ever said, "Why am I so tired today?" "Why am I *still* struggling with this?" "Why am I not over that yet?" "Why am I like this?" "Why am I so emotional?" "I need to do better . . . be better . . ."?

Maybe it'd be good for you to be kind to yourself. You're living in a moving, breathing picture. You're not going to remain the same and you're still growing. Releasing the past to be able to build our future takes intention, but it also requires us to walk in God's grace to be able to move forward and trust where He's leading us.

When we first moved to Charleston, I was frustrated. No longer being on the hamster wheel in the City That Never Sleeps was both welcome and terrifying. I had gotten used to juggling co-leading a church alongside my husband, leading a women's conference in the city, traveling and speaking to the greater church in different cities and nations, writing books for my publisher, hosting my podcast, as well as raising four kids, keeping our marriage healthy and alive, managing a home—oh, and trying to stay spiritually, physically, mentally, and emotionally strong. *Busy* had become my unintentional badge of honor. The logistical move from Brooklyn to Charleston did a number on me internally. There's a sacred slowness that rests on Charleston as the salty air from the Atlantic Ocean hovers over the interconnected wetlands we now call home. Just existing in our new postal code slowed me right down, quieting the buzz that had been right there under my skin the twelve years prior.

Many of my initial prayers in the first months living in South Carolina were laden with repentance. Repentance that I had found any measure of my identity in what I did or could accomplish. I was no longer leading a church or a women's conference. My podcast was on hiatus for an unknown period of time. I kept hearing the Holy Spirit nudge me: *Surrender ... surrender all. Rest. Surrender. Let go...* The truth was, I had entered a season that I'd prayed for. I had less to do and plenty of time to surrender and trust. I had an innate knowing that this was a time of healing and rest to be able to build our future. Liminal spaces can be hard, brimming with unanswered questions, but they are necessary for our rest and growth.

So be kind to yourself. Take a breath and lay claim to (or reclaim) a rhythm of rest. And if you find yourself in what feels like a forced season of rest, don't rush the process. You are in a sacred space. Be present and simply ask what God wants to do in you.

BUILDING ON THE ROCK

Scripture Meditation: Psalm 23

> The LORD is my shepherd, I lack nothing.
>> He makes me lie down in green pastures,
> he leads me beside quiet waters,
>> he refreshes my soul.
> He guides me along the right paths
>> for his name's sake.
> Even though I walk
>> through the darkest valley,

183

I will fear no evil,
for you are with me;
your rod and your staff,
they comfort me.

You prepare a table before me
in the presence of my enemies.
You anoint my head with oil;
my cup overflows.
Surely your goodness and love will follow me
all the days of my life,
and I will dwell in the house of the LORD
forever.

Take a moment. Read the passage out loud. What hits different for you in this season? Where do you need fresh revelation?

REFLECTION QUESTIONS

- Do you have an established rhythm of rest? If yes, what does it look like for you week to week? And if not, what is your biggest hurdle to finding one?
- What new understanding (if any) can you take and implement from reading about Sabbath?

GUIDED PRAYER

Father, thank You for creating a way for me to abide with You daily in trust and intimacy through the life, death, and resurrection of Jesus and the subsequent gift of the Holy Spirit. Jesus, You have the ability to give me rest as I choose to intimately connect with You. Forgive me for the times that I have rejected Your perfect plan and instead chosen to toil, tethered to the ways of the world. I submit my life once again to You as the Good Shepherd and ask that You would lead, refresh, and guide me along the right paths for the glory of Your name. I trust You with my whole life and know that You accomplish more on my day of rest than I ever could in six days of work. Speak to me by Your Spirit and show me the rhythm of rest You have mapped out for me in the particular season I'm in right now. I give You my plans and ask that You replace them with Yours.

CHAPTER 10

A TIME TO REBUILD

Nobody can go back and start a new beginning, but anyone
can start today and make a new ending.

Maria Robinson

Paul's dad, Greg, stood in the middle of our street, waving goodbye to us as the sun set over our Brooklyn brownstone. It was
heartbreaking to watch him standing there alone as we drove off
into our new life. All six of us were sobbing, not a single one of us
had any intention of holding back. We let the grief wash over us.
We'd built a beautiful life in New York for twelve years and were
leaving it all behind: the church we'd planted, Paul's dad, the city
we'd raised our babies in, our friends, the victories and failures,
the memories. We were leaving it all on the field, so to speak, and
it ached. It still does if I sit with it for too long.

We drove past the kids' elementary school; our local pizza
place with the perfect greasy slice; the bagel shop right by our
subway stop; our neighborhood bodega (a small convenience

store), Frank's, also known as my kids' favorite place to spend their allowance. I even shed a tear for Rite Aid because it held so many memories for us, the toy aisle specifically. Directly across the street from Rite Aid was our park, which held countless moments that we'll never forget: The summer and autumn birthday parties at the picnic tables and the snow days spent building tiny snowmen alongside our neighbors, who were also dragging a kid or two behind them on plastic sleds that broke after the first or second use. The hot slides that sizzled the kids' exposed thighs and calves in the summertime, which they went down time and time again, despite the burn. The kids waiting their turn in long lines to get three minutes on the swing and running through the sprinklers in the sweltering heat, slathered in sunscreen, wearing Crocs, and screaming with delight as the cooling mist made contact with their sweet faces.

As all the memories hit, the grief rolled over us like a twenty-foot wave. There was no stopping it, the hard and the good memories, the reality of what we were losing as we drove toward all that we were about to gain. Starting over is hard.

Halfway between Brooklyn and Charleston, we let ourselves listen to "Starting Over" by Chris Stapleton. If you haven't heard it, do yourself a favor and have a listen. It was quiet in the car as we took in the scenery around us, letting the words overwhelm our senses. I gripped Paul's hand as we both wiped tears from our eyes, holding tightly to one another, braving the change we were embarking on. One of the verses looks forward with understanding that it may not be easy to start over, alluding to the reality that there will be days when we'll absolutely fall apart and walk through dark valleys but that one day we'll look back and be glad we said yes to the change laid out before us.

Months earlier, we'd come to Charleston to "spy out the land." By the end of our trip, we'd known this was going to be the place we'd settle our family in the coming months. As we flew off into the sunset on our way back to New York, I had started to wonder how we'd do it: How would we uproot our kids and move again? How would we set up a new home, make new friends, settle into new schools, and build a new life? How would we start over?

As the sun set over the twisting and bending marshland, the sky glowing a warm burnt orange with streaks of fiery red and splashes of pink, in my pondering I heard the Lord whisper clear as anything, *I am your home*. No matter where we are on the earth, He is our home and our hope. The center of it all.

Fast-forward months later to me sitting in our furnished rental, and I heard it again: *I am your home. I've got you right where I want you*. I decided to sit in the peace of that moment, in the tenderness of God nudging me with a promise, reminding me of His never-ending presence. He is my firm foundation, unshakable through the shaking. He is the One on which I choose to build my home and my life, and in Him is where I put my hope. So, whether I am beginning again, recovering from a loss, facing a difficult ending or situation, or walking into a new season, He is my home. My Rock.

As you read these words, how does this apply to you right here, right now? Maybe take some time to sit in God's presence. Cry out for understanding or surrender the need to control the outcomes. Open your palms to heaven, close your eyes, lean in, and listen. Find rest and peace in the present moment you find yourself in, even in the wondering and the waiting. He is with you.

I've learned that it's difficult to begin again or embrace change unless we're willing to release the past, grow through the process, and continually surrender all, trusting that God is holding us by the hand and leading us on paths of righteousness for His name's sake.

DEATH IN THE SPIRITUAL CAN BRING NEW LIFE

I'd slept heavily. Like, I didn't move from the position I'd fallen asleep in until I woke early the next morning. And even though I'd slept like an actual rock, when I looked back at my journal entry from the day before, I saw that I'd written that I'd felt "sad, heavy, and tired." It was the morning of our final She Is Free board meeting. The meeting was to close everything down that I'd pioneered for the women of Liberty Church (the church my husband and I had planted in New York City in 2010) starting in 2014. Leading She Is Free was an act of obedience for me, and I laid it down every year, asking God if He wanted me to pick it back up. It existed to engage and equip women to encounter God and expand the Kingdom in their spheres of influence. We'd seen so many women saved, healed, and delivered over a five-year period. So, when it became clear that our commission in New York was done, I'd wondered what I was supposed to do with She Is Free.

My friend Irene and I had just decided that we'd merge our passions to see women set free and lead the movement together into the next season. We'd had such fresh vision and anticipation around it all, and then, over the exact same period of time, both of our lives entirely changed. Jimmy and Irene as well as Paul and I knew it was time to transition the churches we'd both pastored over to new leadership. Within a few months of one another, we passed the figurative batons over to new pastors. Before this all took place, we'd filmed videos for the future of She Is Free, had planning meetings with our team, set up a 501(c)(3), created a new website, started strategizing our next steps, and then it was as if the road ran out or the brook dried up. It was confusing. We had felt that the prophetic word over that year for She Is Free was "new thing" from Isaiah 43:18–19:

Forget the former things;
  do not dwell on the past.
See, I am doing a new thing!
  Now it springs up; do you not perceive it?
  I am making a way in the wilderness
  and streams in the wasteland.

After all of the difficulty that had come out of the prior years, we were expectant for the "new thing" that we believed God wanted to do. Little did we know just how *new* the new thing would be for us. Jimmy and Irene and Paul and I were (and are) the best of friends, with endless passion to see people walk in freedom, but in that particular moment in time, God was carving out a new direction for Jimmy and Irene's life as well as ours. He was doing a new thing in our families, and we were aware that we needed to be obedient, even if people looking on scratched their heads and wondered why.

So instead of doing anything rash (which is more my wheel-house than Irene's), we decided to give it a year, seek God, settle our families in our new respective cities, and then decide on how to move forward with She Is Free. Every time I sought God and asked, "What do you want us to do with She Is Free?" He said the same thing: *Serve the church you're in.* And when I say that's all I heard every time I asked, I mean Every. Single. Time. No deviation.

But that didn't change the fact that this all felt like a death—and a death that deep down I knew was coming. Having that final board meeting to close the doors on what was, and even what could've been, was one of those hard and yet good things we all have to do from time to time: *let go of what was to hold on appropriately to what is.* To be able to walk without hindrance into what is to come. Irene and I realized that we could no longer move forward in the old vehicle; God was giving us both something new.

As we concluded the final meeting, a sense of relief rested on us. We crossed over into the new, making ourselves completely available. We never know what miracles God will do until we consecrate ourselves and walk in obedience.

The night of our last board meeting, I went over to a friend's house in Charleston. When I walked in, she gave me a gift: a new note-taking Bible. She wrote these words in the front: "God is doing a new thing. We will see revival in our time. I love you." I just sat there with wide-eyed wonder. Obedience to let go, surrender, and step into what is next, even when it doesn't make logical sense, makes room for God to do what only He can do.

I often wonder what it must've been like for Joshua to lead Israel into the promised land. The book of Joshua starts out with, "Moses my servant is dead. *Now then*, you and all these people, get ready to cross the Jordan River into the land I am about to give to them—to the Israelites" (Josh. 1:2). God was doing a new thing, with a new leader, with a new generation of Israelites. In essence, they were to "forget the former things" to be able to move into what God had for them, but a lot of times the former things play like an incessant song on repeat in our minds if we don't obey God's nudge to move on. I've heard it said that delayed obedience is disobedience. Moses and a whole generation died in the desert due to continued disobedience, and now it was Joshua's charge to lead them into their promise.

We can garner an abundance of wisdom from Joshua's humble leadership. Right before they marched around Jericho,

> Joshua told the people, "*Consecrate yourselves*, for tomorrow the Lord will do amazing things among you."
> Joshua said to the priests, "*Take up the ark of the covenant and pass on ahead of the people.*" So they took it up and went ahead of them.

And the LORD said to Joshua, "Today I will begin to exalt you in the eyes of all Israel, so they may know that I am with you as I was with Moses. Tell the priests who carry the ark of the covenant: *'When you reach the edge of the Jordan's waters, go and stand in the river.'"*

. . . So when the people broke camp to cross the Jordan, the priests carrying the ark of the covenant went ahead of them. *Now the Jordan is at flood stage all during harvest. Yet as soon as the priests who carried the ark reached the Jordan and their feet touched the water's edge, the water from upstream stopped flowing.* It piled up in a heap a great distance away, at a town called Adam in the vicinity of Zarethan, while the water flowing down to the Sea of the Arabah (that is, the Dead Sea) was completely cut off. So the people crossed over opposite Jericho. *The priests who carried the ark of the covenant of the LORD stopped in the middle of the Jordan and stood on dry ground, while all Israel passed by until the whole nation had completed the crossing on dry ground.* (Josh. 3:5–8, 14–17)

As Joshua led the people into what was new, they had to let go of what was, and before they did, he told them to consecrate themselves because the Lord was about to do amazing miracles among them. The word *consecrate* comes from the Hebrew word *qadash*, which means to be "set apart, holy, or sacred" or to "prepare or dedicate" oneself.[1] There would have been sacrifices being made and ceremonial washings taking place as they entered into holy preparation for all that was to come. Are we in a place where we are prepared and set apart for what God desires to do in and through us? Have we been obedient to let go of the things He has asked us to let go of? Have we surrendered the things that have held us back so that we can move forward?

We then see Joshua tell the priests to take the ark of the covenant ahead of the people. This reminds me that there will be times in life when we'll have to take the lead and move before anyone else makes a move. The Jordan River was at flood stage, so in the natural realm, it wasn't an "ideal" time to prepare and cross over. Yet God doesn't tend to call us into something new when the conditions are perfect, does He? He often leads us into something new when the waters of our lives are at flood stage, where we have to completely trust Him to lead us through.

The priests obey the next thing Joshua tells them to do, which is to carry the ark of the covenant and step into the middle of the flooded river. So they carry the presence and the promises of God into a dangerous river, with faith that God will come through—and He does. The moment the priests have their feet in the river, the water from upstream stops flowing. The priests step into the middle of the riverbed, on dry ground, until the whole nation of Israel has crossed over. This whole passage makes me think about how often we must choose to brave the changes in front of us, even when others may not want to. So pause for a moment and recall the times you've trusted God and let go of what was and possibly stepped into a liminal space before anyone else, believing that He'd show up and, in turn, make a way for others to walk through.

We can understand through Scripture and experience that death in the spiritual brings new life. We have to be willing to let go of something that was great but is no longer good for us and not our responsibility to carry. We cannot rebuild and say yes to the new assignment God is placing before us if we're still gripping on to what was. Life is full of moments when we let go and then pick up the right things . . . tear down and uproot, rebuild, and replant. We have to release the past to be able to build the future.

UPROOT AND PLANT

I've observed many self-proclaimed social media "prophets" uprooting, tearing down, destroying, overthrowing, holding to account, and flipping over tables (out of biblical context) in the name of Jesus. Our God is a restoring God, and we see this throughout the Old and New Testaments. If we stop at tearing down and uprooting what was, we'll be left with a desolate city and fruitless garden. In Jeremiah 1:10, God says to Jeremiah,

> See, today I appoint you over nations and kingdoms to *uproot* and *tear down*, to *destroy* and *overthrow*, to *build* and to *plant*.

In context, Jeremiah has just been called as a young prophet to the nation of Israel. Throughout the book of Jeremiah, he prophesies of his people's imminent exile to Babylon because of their refusal to turn from sin, but he also prophesies the forthcoming fall of Babylon and the promise of God's gracious restorative salvation. True to the command God gave him at the inauguration of his calling, he does the work of uprooting and tearing down, as well as declaring the destruction of a people. Not an easy mission! But he doesn't leave it there; he also "builds" and "plants" with his words in obedience to the word of the Lord. In Jeremiah 31:33, God speaks of the grace to come:

> "This is the covenant I will make with the people of Israel
>   after that time," declares the LORD.
> "I will put my law in their minds
>   and write it on their hearts.
> I will be their God,
>   and they will be my people."

If we only uproot, tear down, destroy, and overthrow with our words and actions in the midst of national change and tragedy or deeply personal life transitions, loss, or endings, we will live in a physical and spiritual wasteland. There is a tension here. Once the soil is void of seed, weeds, or crops due to "uprooting" and the walls have been torn down of what used to be, we need to start the work of replanting and rebuilding—it is both/and. Living in a perpetual state of ruminating on what was, finding flaws, or pointing fingers will be detrimental to you and those left in your wake in the end. At some stage, we'll wake up with amnesia, forgetting the continual grace of God that has been poured out over our lives, and be found in an unending cycle of fear and anxiety. We must make the choice to set about the work of intentional rebuilding and replanting to establish the Kingdom of God here on earth as it is in heaven.

REBUILD WHAT'S RIGHT IN FRONT OF YOU

Once everything has changed, where do we even begin to rebuild or, in some cases, start building?

Nehemiah 3 is a favorite of mine. But before we get there, let's get some context. In chapter 1, Nehemiah learns that those who survived the Babylonian exile (prophesied by Jeremiah) are in disgrace and that the walls of Jerusalem have been broken down and burned (vv. 1–3). Nehemiah weeps and mourns, fasts and prays, asking God what he can do to rebuild the city that has his heart. At the time, he is a cupbearer to King Artaxerxes, so when he brings wine to the king in chapter 2, the king observes that something is wrong with Nehemiah . . . that he has a great sadness hovering over him. Nehemiah boldly tells the king of his heartache and asks for permission and favor to leave, go back to Jerusalem, and rebuild the walls of his broken-down city. The king not only grants him permission but sends him with letters for building materials and safe passage, as well as a cavalry and army officers.

When Nehemiah gets to Jerusalem, he's slow to tell others what God has put in his heart to do. He holds it close, pondering the task that is in front of him. He observes the walls that have been broken down and the gates that have been destroyed by fire and then says to the Jews, priests, nobles, officials, and those who will be doing the work,

> "You see the trouble we are in: Jerusalem lies in ruins, and its gates have been burned with fire. *Come, let us rebuild* the wall of Jerusalem, and we will no longer be in disgrace." I also told them about the gracious hand of my God on me and what the king had said to me.
>   They replied, *"Let us start rebuilding."* *So they began this good work.* (2:17–18)

And then in chapter 3 we see the rebuilding beginning to take place. When you read it, you may just see a bunch of names, but I see something miraculous. The phrases "next to them," "next to him," and "next to that" are repeated over and over again. The people of the city walked out of their houses and rebuilt the broken-down wall that was right in front of them. Shoulder to shoulder, with charred stones, they were obedient to rebuild that which had been devastated, and fifty-two days later, the wall was complete. Because one man—Nehemiah—decided to ask after his people. And when the answer broke his heart, he took time to fast, weep, and pray, and God led him to action. He was obedient and went before the king to ask permission to set his hand to this good work of restoration. The king not only said yes but granted him favor. When he arrived on assignment, he didn't come in with all guns blazing. Instead, he took a moment to observe the damage and the work that needed to be done. And then he didn't do it alone; he gathered his people, and they rebuilt together.

What is God asking you to lament, weep, fast, and pray over? Where is He asking you to stop and survey the damage and assess the work that needs to be done? Who is He asking you to stand next to as you rebuild (or begin to build) what's right in front of you?

As you set out in obedience, trusting that God is with you, know this: resistance is a reality that comes with the territory. Right after Nehemiah calls the people to rebuild, Sanballat and Tobiah show up on the scene to launch an ongoing campaign to mock, discredit, ridicule, discourage, strike fear into, deter, and ultimately stop Nehemiah from rebuilding the wall. He is met with opposition but doesn't allow it to take him off mission. From Moses to the nation of Israel to the prophets to Jesus and His disciples (including you and me), resistance is a reality to those who are on mission.

And when we get resistance, we resist right back. James 4:7 says, "Submit yourselves, then, to God. *Resist* the devil, and he will flee from you." Submission to God first and foremost gives us the authority to resist the devil in Jesus's name.

FIX YOUR EYES

Having clear vision is imperative as we brave change. In chapter 2, I wrote about labor being a part of life. How the incessant pain of things shifting, ceasing, and changing around us and in our relationships can cause us to feel like we're incapable of moving forward. And just as a woman rocking, shaking, and crying out in labor and moving into the transition stage needs a vision that the level of pain she's experiencing will soon cease, and she'll be looking upon the face of her child—so do we. I had seen each of my kids' squishy bodies and tiny profiles on ultrasounds, but I hadn't yet met them face-to-face. As transition hit my body in the final stages of labor, to stay present and move through it, I pictured the moment of meeting them, of seeing their created form. I had a vision for what was to come through the pain, that joy would come on the other side of this labor. It kept me focused and single-minded, moving with the natural rhythm of my body.

Hebrews 11:1 says, "Now faith is the substance of things hoped for, the evidence of things not seen" (NKJV). With this being true, then I'd say making the choice to trust where God is leading us through the pain of change is worth every step. Every tear. Every prayer. Every hour of waiting, wondering, and hoping.

Hebrews 11 goes on to say,

> For by it the elders obtained a good testimony.
> By faith we understand that the worlds were framed by the word of God, so that the things which are seen were not made of things which are visible. (vv. 2–3 NKJV)

The "it" in "For by it" refers to faith: this is how the elders that have gone before us obtained a good testimony, one of integrity and honor. The New International Version says that "this is what the ancients were commended for" (v 2), in other words, what they were praised and remembered for. We can look back through the Bible at all of the elders of our faith and see that they held on to hope, whether they saw a promise come to pass in their lifetime or not They knew the God they served was omnipotent and sovereign. Hebrews 11 is the "by faith" chapter: "By faith Abel . . . By faith Enoch . . . By faith Noah . . . By faith Abraham . . . By faith Sarah . . ." and so on. They lived *by faith* because they had an understanding that the very ground they stood on, that *we* stand on, was created from the "Let there be . . ." straight from the mouth of God. Things that were not in existence came into existence as God spoke. Our ancestors had an understanding that whatever trials they went through would be outweighed by the eternal glory of God that will last forever and that it's impossible to please God when we live without faith (Heb. 11:6). Why? Because trust in ourselves and our abilities will ultimately run dry if it's more than our trust in a good and loving Father who knows exactly what we need. Our endeavors will eventually fail, and our talents will only take us so far. So why wouldn't we trust in Him and Him alone, even when we don't understand or can't make things work according to our plans and even when we perceive that things are all going our way?

So, in light of this, let us *fix our eyes* on the Author and Finisher of our faith, the One who rides through every storm with us while remaining securely enthroned over all of creation. Every change around us is an opportunity to bring Christlike and eternal change within us. As 2 Corinthians 3:18 says, we "are being transformed into his image with ever-increasing glory, which comes from the Lord, who is the Spirit." And because of this reality, we don't lose heart.

In 2 Corinthians 4, the apostle Paul reminds us of the goodness of God's mercy that causes us to renounce our "secret and shameful ways" (v. 2) because the light of the world has come to make His home within us. So when we are crushed and pressed on every side, when the storm bruises and batters our lives, we'll remember what we've built our lives on and just who lives within us.

> But we have this treasure in jars of clay to show that this all-surpassing power is from God and not from us. *We are hard pressed on every side, but not crushed; perplexed, but not in despair; persecuted, but not abandoned; struck down, but not destroyed. We always carry around in our body the death of Jesus, so that the life of Jesus may also be revealed in our body.* For we who are alive are always being given over to death for Jesus' sake, so that his life may also be revealed in our mortal body. So then, death is at work in us, but life is at work in you. (vv. 7–12)

To me, this is such a picture of life. Pressing, crushing, perplexity, loss, pain, persecution, battles . . . Remembering that we are crucified with Christ—that we "carry around in our body the death of Jesus" so that His life may be revealed there also. Whatever we go through, Christ can be revealed through us!

> *Therefore we do not lose heart.* Though outwardly we are wasting away, yet inwardly we are being renewed day by day. For our light and momentary troubles are achieving for us an eternal glory that far outweighs them all. *So we fix our eyes* not on what is seen, but on what is unseen, since what is seen is temporary, but what is unseen is eternal. (vv. 16–18)

So where have you fixed your eyes? This will determine our outcomes, health, heart posture, and trajectory more than we know. Are our eyes fixed on what is seen, that which will fade away? Or are they fixed on the unseen, the eternal, that which will remain?

We need vision in transition coupled with a passionate resolve to fix our eyes on Jesus, come what may.

REMEMBER, *HE* MAKES ALL THINGS NEW

There's a worship song I love to play and yell-sing in my car or at home alone, especially the chorus, which states that God can do anything. I literally yell, "YOU CAN DO ANYTHING!" along with the rest of the chorus and fist-pump the air with the hand not holding the steering wheel. If I'm at a stoplight, you better believe that both hands are free to go wild while I give my driving neighbors a good laugh. Listen, the caps and exclamation marks are necessary here. God can actually do anything. He can and will make all things new. He is a God of hope, transformation, restoration, and resurrection. And, most likely, He will *not* make all things new according to our plan, because He is Lord and King, and we are not. There's real freedom in that truth.

Here are four biblical references to how God makes all things new:

1. Israel's Only Savior

> Forget the former things;
>   do not dwell on the past.
> See, *I am doing a new thing!*
>   Now it springs up; do you not perceive it?
> I am making a way in the wilderness
>   and streams in the wasteland. (Isa. 43:18–19)

The book of Isaiah is full of messianic prophecy. Even though Israel has turned away and been unfaithful to God time and again, He pledges that He will once again send His mercy. This *new thing* that we read about in verse 19 is a prophetic word pointing to the long-awaited Messiah. The reality is, we are living in this promise today. He has made all things new in and through Christ Jesus, our Messiah.

How does the reality of this promise speak to you in times of rebuilding and transition?

_____

_____

_____

_____

2. New Mercies Every Morning

> The steadfast love of the LORD never ceases;
> *his mercies never come to an end;*
> *they are new every morning;*
> great is your faithfulness. (Lam. 3:22–23 ESV)

Even as we lament and walk through hardship, it's good to remember that His mercies are new every single morning. As you wake in the morning, take a deep breath and call to mind this truth: He is good and present with you in the uncomfortable and difficult liminal spaces of life.

How does the truth that "His mercies never come to an end" transform you, even as you lament and grieve? How can you embrace the newness of mercy daily?

_____

_____

_____

_____

3. Dead to Sin, Made New and Alive in Christ

We were buried therefore with him by baptism into death, in order that, just as Christ was raised from the dead by the glory of the Father, we too might walk in *newness of life*. (Rom. 6:4 ESV)

Newness of life comes as we submit our lives, crucify the flesh, and pick up our cross to follow Christ daily. Remember what Jesus said to His disciples: "Whoever wants to be my disciple must deny themselves and take up their cross and follow me.

For whoever wants to save their life will lose it, but whoever loses their life for me will find it" (Matt. 16:24–25).

How does your perspective change when you let go of what you thought life should or would be like and instead choose to embrace the cross?

_____

_____

_____

_____

4. A New Heaven and a New Earth

And he who was seated on the throne said, *"Behold, I am making all things new."* Also he said, "Write this down, for these words are trustworthy and true." (Rev. 21:5 ESV)

This speaks to the final coming of the King of Heaven here on earth . . . The restoration of Eden, the New Jerusalem. When Jesus returns as King, He will deal with evil forever and vindicate those who have been faithful to Him. He will live with humanity, healing the pain of evil, restoring creation, and making all things new. God's presence will permeate every inch of the earth, and a new humanity will fulfill the original calling in Genesis to rule and reign on earth.

This is the ultimate restoration that our salvation points to. This is how we fix our eyes on what is eternal when the external pressures feel like they could crush us under their weight. He is making all things new.

How does the promise of our coming King help you to fix your eyes on what is unseen instead of that which is seen?

_____

_____

_____

_____

JESUS, THE ONLY CONSTANT

Let's finish where we started: the Sermon on the Mount.

A sermon that illustrates how the gospel of the Kingdom of Heaven will come to earth. A sermon that is the fulfillment of the law through Christ (Matt. 5:17–18) yet is still impossible to live without Him. It's a sermon that invites His disciples to live according to the coming Kingdom within this present broken and hurting world. These teachings are essential for those who *choose* to live in the light of His lordship in and through every season.

Let's read the culmination of this pivotal sermon one last time together.

Therefore *everyone who hears these words of mine and puts them into practice is like a wise man who built his house on the rock*. The rain came down, the streams rose, and the winds blew and beat against that house; yet it did not fall, *because it had its foundation on the rock*. But everyone who hears these words of mine and does not put them into practice is like a foolish man who built his house on sand. The rain came down, the streams rose, and the winds blew and beat against that house, and it fell with a great crash. (Matt. 7:24–27)

Braving change is not for the faint of heart, but you've done it before, and you will continue to move through it with grace as you choose to build your foundation upon the Rock. Because we know that life is full of change: the good, painful, and disappointing kinds. Forced change, national change, and even hope-filled change. We'll have plenty of uncomfortable change and political change as kingdoms continue to rise and fall. We'll make necessary changes and at times be shocked by the uncontrollable and traumatic changes we face. There will be surprising change, joy-filled change, the "choices we need to make as we age" kind of change, and of course, desired change. It is a constant force. The rains will come, the streams will rise, and the winds will beat against our lives, and even when we're shaken, the Rock we stand on will remain steadfast and immovable. As you continue to brave the waters of change, remember that, above all, Christ Jesus is our only constant, our firm foundation.

When you cry out for change, recognize transition when you're in it, grieve, and recover from the losses, may you *release the past* and forget the former things as God does something new in and through you. I pray that you'd openly *welcome growth* and transformation in the light of His love, surrendering all with a childlike faith, *trusting where God is leading you.*

BUILDING ON THE ROCK

Scripture Meditation: Matthew 5–7

In your own time, read the Sermon on the Mount in its fullness. If you can, linger and take it all in. Ask the Holy Spirit to empower you to live it as you continue to brave the changes ahead of you.

REFLECTION QUESTIONS

- Are you available to surrender when God says let go? Available to get up and move with just a nudge of His Spirit?
- Are your hands open to whatever He wants to do?

GUIDED PRAYER

This time, I'll have you write your own prayer to God. Start with gratitude and go from there. What has He done in you? What has He spoken to you? Are you still frustrated and confused? What questions do you have? What are your hopes? What are you excited about? Don't hold back; cry out to Him and thank Him for being with you always.

_____

_____

_____

_____

_____

_____

_____

_____

_____

_____

_____

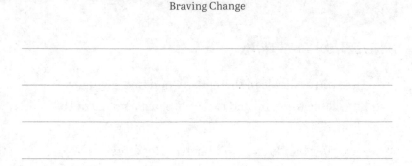

MY FINAL PRAYER FOR YOU FROM PHILIPPIANS 1

I am certain that God, who began the good work within you, will continue his work until it is finally finished on the day when Christ Jesus returns . . .

I pray that your love will overflow more and more, and that you will keep on growing in knowledge and understanding. For I want you to understand what really matters, so that you may live pure and blameless lives until the day of Christ's return. May you always be filled with the fruit of your salvation—the righteous character produced in your life by Jesus Christ—for this will bring much glory and praise to God.

Philippians 1:6, 9–11 NLT

ACKNOWLEDGMENTS

Paul, thank you for giving me space to write, create, edit, edit, and edit some more, time and time again. I know I basically disappear for months on end when I start a new writing project, and you pick up the slack in areas I don't even notice or see—so thank you for that too. You're an exceptional husband and father . . . intentional, selfless, up for an adventure, supportive, and always willing to pivot. Thank you for seeing me, releasing me, and loving me no matter what, even when I can be a handful. I have always felt deeply known and loved by you.

Zeke, Jesse, Finley, and Sam, there are not enough words to say thank you for legitimately being the greatest joy of Dad's and my life. I love being your mom more than any other "job" I've ever been given. You are each so brilliantly unique, deeply connected, kind, intelligent, and creative. I often pinch myself realizing once again that it's not a dream; I get to do life with each of you. You make parenting so much fun, and I can genuinely say that each stage of raising you has been my "favorite" because I get to watch you grow and change before my very eyes. Thank you for giving me space once again to write this book. I pray that one day when you need them most, the words in these pages will be right on time for your hungry heart.

Tanya, thank you for reading different chapters and giving honest feedback before I sent the first draft off to Rebekah. Your suggestions and opinions were extremely valuable. On top of that, I am exceedingly grateful for you as a human being in my life. Year after year, you've been a steady, loving friend. We've been through countless seasons together, and this book reflects so many of the lessons learned throughout our twenty-plus years of doing life in various contexts. From Spokane to Sydney to New York to Charleston, more than you'll ever know I value your steadfast love, encouragement, and genuine friendship. They've been an anchor through the toughest of times and a fount of continuous joy whenever we're together.

Kaylee, thank you for reading every single chapter before I turned the manuscript in. The way you know me and saw what needed to be weeded out of different chapters but also what was helpful for the reader and needed to be emphasized even more was a gift. And when my words got petty or personal, you weren't afraid to call it out so I could kindly rephrase (and repent). Going through some of our greatest personal storms simultaneously over the last few years was wild, yet I'm eternally grateful we weathered them together. The Andrew family is officially a Kaylee Morgan fan for life. I can't believe our worlds divinely collided when they did, and I will always be thankful to God for it.

Irene, thank you for the major contributions you have allowed me to use in "Choose Integrity in Change" because, my goodness, you live it. That phone call with you was so life-giving, and I know that the words I wrote directly from your mouth at the start of the chapter will be a road map for countless readers. Beyond that, I am thankful for your friendship. The way you love is just like Jesus, and it's changed me. Year after year, it's such a joy to be friends who get to grow together as we continue to choose to "do the work." Thank you for continuing to tenderly speak the truth in love to me. I'm in your corner forever, friend.

Josh, Lisa, Jason, and Jenna, I'll never forget that night on the porch in May of 2022 when Paul and I vulnerably opened up our lives, and instead of creating distance, you welcomed us even closer with open arms. Honestly, I'm not sure where Paul and I would be without your love and friendship as we navigated such a major transition with our family. Instead of feeling lost at sea, we found home. It's not lost on me that I had the privilege of writing the words of this book while tucked into the safety of new and loving friendships that changed so many of my perspectives.

Lisa and Jenna, I never knew that I could feel seen and safe so quickly. You are helping me unlearn and relearn things in friendship that I didn't even know I needed until now. It's been so healing, not to mention fun! I can't believe that God would be so kind as to allow us to do life together, and I'm not sad about it. Here's to great and wonderful days ahead. Love you all, or y'all, so much.

Greg and Debbie, your "yes" to move to Charleston all those years ago has changed the trajectory of our family's lives. Thank you for creating a space for so many people to find Jesus and thrive in community, including us all these years later. The way you love and see people, know them by name, and create spaces to heal is unlike any ecosystem we've ever been in. It's unique, powerful, centered on Jesus, and bringing healing to countless lives. "Thank you" doesn't even begin to express our gratitude.

Kathy, thank you for reading the words in this book and giving honest feedback on title ideas before we settled on *Braving Change*. You are such a gift to the body of Christ but, personally, to my life as well. Thank you for receiving me with joy and cheering me on. I love that I get to now do life with you!

Rebekah, I was so nervous when you came out to visit me in Charleston to talk about the future of my writing career and relationship with Baker Books. Okay, that's a tad dramatic (as you and I both know I can be), but we'd just moved our family, and my whole life was up in the air. In my (now obvious to me) insecurity, I wasn't sure you'd want to continue to work with me, to which you said, "Why do you think I flew out here? I'd love to keep working with you, and so would Baker." Or something to that effect. Either way, from our first book together, I have felt seen by you. You understand me and my voice and encourage me to keep getting the lines on the page, to remain faithful to what's in my heart to write. Thank you for flying out so that you, Tanya, and I could workshop this book together. I do think we need to do it with the next one too. I'm so excited to see where *Braving Change* will go, but more than ever, I am just so grateful to run alongside you. Thank you for your continual belief in me. Also, I really just love hanging out with you.

NOTES

Chapter 1 The Change We Think We Want

1. *CSB Everyday Study Bible* (Nashville: Holman Bible Publishers, 2018; CSB Text Revision, 2020), footnote, p. 1217.
2. M. Scott Peck, *The Road Less Traveled: A New Psychology of Love, Traditional Values, and Spiritual Growth, 25th Anniversary Edition* (New York: Simon and Schuster, 2002), 15.

Chapter 2 Recognize Transition When You're in It

1. Oxford Languages, s.v. "plateau," accessed April 21, 2023, https://www.google.com/search?q=plateau.
2. The editors of *Encyclopaedia Britannica*, s.v. "grace," Britannica, last updated April 7, 2023, https://www.britannica.com/topic/grace-religion.
3. Oxford Languages, s.v. "grace," accessed April 21, 2023, https://www.google.com/search?q=grace.

Chapter 3 The Need to Grieve and Give Yourself Permission to Change

1. William Cowper, "Charity," *Poems by William Cowper, of the Inner Temple, Esq.*, line 159.
2. The stages themselves are from "The 7 Stages of Grief and How They Affect You" by the BetterHelp Editorial Team and medically reviewed by Aaron Dutil, LMHC, LPC, BetterHelp, updated April 3, 2023, https://www.betterhelp.com/advice/grief/the-7-stages-of-grief-and-how-they-affect-you/; the paraphrase of each stage is my own.
3. "7 Stages of Grief," BetterHelp.
4. Whitney Woollard, "Lamentations: The Volatile Voice of Grief," BibleProject, accessed March 2, 2023, https://bibleproject.com/blog/lamentations-voice-of-grief/.

Chapter 4 A Time to Recover

1. Oxford Languages, s.v. "recover," accessed March 23, 2023, https://www.google.com/search?q=recover.
2. EMDR stands for Eye Movement Desensitization and Reprocessing. For more information, read *Getting Past Your Past* by Francine Shapiro, PhD, the originator and developer of EMDR.
3. "Issue Pamphlets," Resources, Celebrate Recovery, accessed March 23, 2023, celebraterecovery.com/resources/issue-pamphlets.
4. For more information and resources, see Stuart Greer's *Freedom, Healing & Deliverance*, https://www.stuartgreer.org/.
5. Oxford Languages, s.v. "stronghold," accessed March 23, 2023, https://www.google.com/search?q=stronghold.

Chapter 5 Learning from Change

1. From Biography.com editors, "B.B. King," last updated August 26, 2020, https://www.biography.com/musicians/bb-king.
2. "Abigail Adams to John Quincy Adams, 20 March 1780," Founders Online, National Archives, https://founders.archives.gov/documents/Adams/04-03-02-0240.
3. Reinhold Niebuhr, "Serenity Prayer," Celebrate Recovery, accessed March 24, 2023, https://www.celebraterecovery.com/resources/serenity-prayer.
4. Niebuhr, "Serenity Prayer."

Chapter 6 Choose to Keep Showing Up

1. Bob Sorge, *Secrets of the Secret Place* (Grandview, MO: Oasis House, 2021), 98.
2. Dietrich Bonhoeffer, *The Cost of Discipleship* (New York: Touchstone, 1995), 88.
3. "Building on the Cornerstone," Back to the Bible, January 23, 2019, https://www.backtothebible.org/post/building-on-the-cornerstone.

Chapter 7 Choose Integrity in Change

1. Oxford Languages, s.v. "integrity," accessed March 28, 2023, https://www.google.com/search?q=integrity.
2. Judson W. Van De Venter, "I Surrender All," 1896, Hymnary.org, accessed March 28, 2023, https://hymnary.org/text/all_to_jesus_i_surrender.
3. Oxford Languages, s.v. "integrity."
4. *Merriam-Webster*, s.v. "subtweet," accessed March 28, 2023, https://www.merriam-webster.com/dictionary/subtweet.
5. "Celebrate Recovery 12 Steps and Biblical Comparisons," Celebrate Recovery, accessed March 28, 2023, https://www.celebraterecovery.com/resources/12-steps.
6. Oxford Languages, s.v. "integrity."

Chapter 8 Choose Gratitude

1. Theodora Blanchfield, "What Is Liminal Space? A Transitional Place or Time That Can Feel Unsettling," Verywell Mind, September 19, 2022, https://www.verywellmind.com/the-impact-of-liminal-space-on-your-mental-health-5204371.

2. Horatio Spafford, "It Is Well with My Soul," 1873, Hymnary.org, accessed June 23, 2023, https://hymnary.org/text/when_peace_like_a_river_attendeth _my_way.

Chapter 9 Choose Rhythms of Rest

1. John Mark Comer, *The Ruthless Elimination of Hurry: How to Stay Emotionally Healthy and Spiritually Alive in the Chaos of the Modern World* (Colorado Springs: WaterBrook, 2019), 155.
2. Missy Takano, "What Is the Sabbath in the Bible and Should Christians Observe It?," BibleProject, accessed March 28, 2023, https://bibleproject.com /blog/keeping-the-sabbath-is-it-still-relevant-to-christians-today/.

Chapter 10 A Time to Rebuild

1. Old Testament Hebrew Lexicon, s.v. "qadash," Bible Study Tools, accessed July 5, 2023, https://www.biblestudytools.com/lexicons/hebrew/kjv/qadash.html #:~:text=kaw%'(Qal).

ABOUT THE AUTHOR

ANDI ANDREW

has been in vocational ministry since 1998. She is the podcast host of *Coffee with Andi* and the author of four books, *She Is Free*, *Fake or Follower*, *Friendship—It's Complicated*, and *Braving Change*, with more projects to come. Passionate about wholeness, family, and creating safe spaces for the prophetic to move, Andi is a heartfelt preacher who loves to see the reality of the gospel worked out in our everyday lives. She and her husband, Paul, planted a family of churches that began in New York City in 2010, which they pastored together for twelve years. In 2021, Paul and Andi began to feel a shift in their assignment. They transitioned the church they'd pioneered and moved in 2022 to Charleston, South Carolina, where Andi's life is currently focused on raising her kids, writing, creating, and investing in local churches and in lives around the world, including serving her local church community, Seacoast Church. The most fulfilling thing in Andi's life besides Jesus are her husband and four kids, Zeke, Jesse, Finley, and Sam.

CONNECT WITH ANDI:

WWW.ANDIANDREW.COM

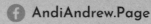 AndiAndrew

 AndiAndrew.Page

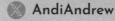 AndiAndrew